CW01637063

'But what are writers *really* like?

'To know that, one must ask them neither for their hangover cures nor for the names of their accountants. One must get them to talk about books. All men may be what they eat; writers alone are what they read. We are all, of course, too *rusés* these sophisticated days to be caught asking a trite question like "read any good books lately?", but it remains, as I believe this book proves, an interesting one to answer, especially for a writer.

'All of those whose answers are to be found in this volume are members, as it happens, of the Writers' Action Group. I was lucky enough to be able to presume on their membership in approaching them. All the proceeds from *Bookmarks* will go to W.A.G.'

FREDERIC RAPHAEL, from his introduction

BOOKMARKS

Edited and Introduced by
FREDERIC RAPHAEL

QUARTET BOOKS LONDON

Published by Quartet Books Limited 1975
27 Goodge Street, London W1P 1FD
simultaneously with Jonathan Cape Limited

ISBN 0 704 31202 6

Printed in Great Britain by
Hunt Barnard Printing Ltd, Aylesbury, Bucks.

CONTENTS

BOOKMARKS

INTRODUCTION

Writers are curious people, in both senses of the word: they are strange and they are inquisitive. As Max Beerbohm's cartoon of Henry James in the hotel corridor rightly warns, they are incorrigible snoopers. It is, I suppose, scarcely surprising that such dedicated sniffers-out should show, in guarding their own privacy, some of the cunning they more commonly devote to quizzing others. How can one ever know what they are really like?

Of course, some authors are much publicized. We get to know of their favourite foods and of their skill in dead-heading roses. We are reassured by their uxorious banality and draw comfort from discovering their reluctance to get on with the job in the morning. But if they are frequently photographed against a background of out-of-focus books, they are seldom encouraged to expand about anything so specialized as literature. Nothing makes an interviewer look more nervously at his watch than literary earnestness. If one wants to make a good impression in the media (and who doesn't?), it is best to discuss sex and wine and to disparage one's friends. Then all may join in. Mention neither art nor money, while seeming to have plenty of both, but not too much of either.

Thus may the writer hope to pass himself off as the *beau idéal* of celebrities: amiable but not patronizing, intelligent but not intellectual, amusing but not facetious, comfortable but unspoiled, witty but not disagreeable. But what are writers *really* like?

To know that, one must ask them neither for their hangover cures nor for the names of their accountants. One must get them to talk about books. All men may be what they eat; writers alone are what they read. We are all, of course, too *rusés* these sophisticated days to be caught asking a trite question like 'Read any good books lately?', but it remains, as I believe this book proves, an interesting one to answer, especially for a writer.

All of those whose answers are to be found in this volume are members, as it happens, of the Writers' Action Group. I was lucky enough to be able to presume on their membership in approaching them. All the royalties from *Bookmarks* will go to W.A.G.

Contrary to suspicious legend, all writers do not know each other. On the contrary, we tend to regard each other with a sort of captious awe. One of the unexpected pleasures, therefore, of editing this book has been in finding out how much I liked those of whom I had for so long been either apprehensive or resentful. Was this the omniscient Mr X and this the caustic Miss Y? How human they were, after all, and how congenial! At the same time, I found that there was hardly a writer whose list of books did not make me conscious of the threadbareness of my own reading. My thanks, therefore, to them all.

FREDERIC RAPHAEL

KINGSLEY AMIS

Louis Armstrong and Tea at Grandma's

I grew up in an environment as unconcerned with literature as most lower middle-class children's must have been in the South London of the years that followed the First World War. My father read detective novels; my mother read romances of the more literate kind; my parents' friends and my friends' parents were similar. There was no local pundit, no opener of my eyes to the magic world of the imagination, and I would as soon have expected to fall in with a Hottentot as with a writer. So, for my friends and me, the written word had the same status as films, records, cricket, the wireless, aeroplanes: irresistibly attractive, to be swallowed whole and unthinkingly.

I never much considered the idea that certain kinds of written-word might be somehow better than others until I was about fourteen, by which time one has done a very large part of one's literary growing-up (as of other kinds of growing-up). To be sure, there was English, there was *The Golden Treasury*, there was Shakespeare, but, as with everything else, that kind of stuff was either instantly like Louis Armstrong and Don Bradman (*Hamlet*) or instantly like museums and tea at Grandma's (*The Merchant of Venice*).

This attitude to literature as to some sort of comestible has a degree of philistinizing effect. I never like to see a book physically ill-treated, however much of a personal *bête noire* its author; but, sentimental reasons apart, I have no interest in anything in its first edition, in its original wrappers, with its original illustrations, numbered and signed by the author, and a paperback, provided I can make it lie flat without breaking its spine, is just lighter and cheaper to replace than its hard-cover version. Type-sizes, quality of paper, binding material mean nothing to me, unless I am the author concerned, which raises a different issue.

Correspondingly, a book—considered now as a piece of literature, not an object—a book that I have to work at, to get into, to read another book about first, etc., is not the book for me. I will not make allowances: what do I care if they liked it that way then because there was no television? If there had been no music, no dancing, no painting, no anything except novels, I would still find Walter Scott insultingly unreadable. He, I imagine, would be on quite a few people's bottom twenty, but for me he is not all that much worse in this regard than Dickens, Jane Austen, Thackeray, most of George Eliot, Hardy's novels, Trollope, James, Conrad, Joyce, Lawrence, Forster. And, of course, no foreigners are to be tolerated; their contribution is merely to give their characters unrememberable names. The novels of the period 1740–1930 (roughly) that come up to Armstrong and Bradman are three by Fielding, two by Smollett, two by Peacock, one and a bit by George Eliot and the first fourty-four pages of one by Joyce. There are also many borderline cases like *Frankenstein, The War of the Worlds, Treasure Island,* of which more in a minute.

I must make it plain that I am not calling Hardy, for instance, a bad novelist; on the contrary, I know that *Jude the Obscure* is a great book, one of the greatest works of art of its splendid century. But its lack of immediacy, however indispensable to the attainment of all its other effects, is still a lack. An example from music may be helpful: nobody would contend that Beethoven's

Second Symphony is as great as his Ninth, and yet it has a freshness that is missing from the later work. I find a faint but distinct air of museums and tea at Grandma's about parts of the Ninth, one that grows less faint in its choral section.

Poetry is a different case: I notice that the first English commentators on it, in the later sixteenth century, insisted on its immediate attractiveness, not as a virtue to be worked for by individual poets, but as a quality inherent in poetry itself. I cannot pretend to be able to swallow the whole of English poetry; nobody could, or should; still, the principle works with remarkable consistency. Anyone failing to be immediately attracted by, say, Tennyson's 'Mariana' must simply hope to be put away somewhere quiet and comfortable, or not too uncomfortable (which is not to say that attractiveness is anywhere near all that poem has to offer). But even the most complex pieces have immediacy too: Donne's *Songs and Sonets, Paradise Lost*. Donne I find myself in the end unable to care for very heartily; *Paradise Lost* is the greatest poem in our language, and the most difficult, and, without being the most attractive, nevertheless undiminishably attractive.

The qualities I have mentioned take some finding in the work of my contemporaries. The test is whether I read and re-read them, not whether I approve of them or whether I would say they were good. By this test, then, I nominate John Betjeman, Philip Larkin, R. S. Thomas, Robert Graves among poets, Evelyn Waugh, Anthony Powell, Elizabeth Taylor among writers of fiction as it is usually thought of, or, by a useful vulgarism, mainstream fiction. But these are far from all the contemporary writers I read and re-read, and here I revert to *Frankenstein* and the other works I called borderline cases.

The borderline is not between the attractive and the less attractive, but between mainstream fiction and, by a necessary clumsiness this time, genre fiction. *Frankenstein* itself has connections with the existing Gothic novel and what was to be science fiction; we today would call *The War of the Worlds* science fiction, though that form of writing had no name even then; *Treasure Island* is a sort of salad, with adventure-tale, historical and 'juvenile' ingredients. Since about the time of its publication in 1883, the genres have expanded to embrace science fiction properly so called, the detective story, the crime novel, the police novel, various kinds of thriller, various tales of horror or terror. It is from among them that I draw a large part of my reading.

Not all of it, naturally, is re-readable, but to be readable at all is a shining virtue, especially these days, when so much mainstream fiction is, besides not being readable, destitute also of those less immediate qualities that arouse respect for nineteenth-century novelists—penetration into character, depth of social understanding and the rest. I will not name names, but the standard modern novel is a self-indulgent moan, a hunk of life neither well observed nor presented in any style, a glum ideological fantasy. Much of the time it reads like a crime novel with no crime, a ghost story with no ghost, a science-fiction story with no science fiction.

Or rather—like a bad example of one of these. In the last twenty years, the genres have attracted writers who would formerly have entered the main stream and distinguished themselves there. Men like Dick Francis, Gavin Lyall, Desmond Bagley, with their counterparts in the other genre forms, move on the level of sophistication and insight that that standard modern novel aspires to without reaching. But I would not re-read them, as I do, were it not for the instant attractions they exerted on me in the first place. If this seems a paradox, it is only because of the puritanical part of our nature, still grumbling that what is really good, or good for us, cannot make an immediate appeal. So ran the objections to poetry four hundred years ago.

PAUL BAILEY

I spent the summer of my seventeenth year reading all the novels of Turgenev. I remember with great clarity the effect they had upon me. I think it was the seemingly effortless construction of the narratives which moved me most: an art so perfect one forgot it was art. I knew then that I would be a writer of fiction one day, even though I was training to become an actor. I already had a yearning to build something that would last.

Many good novelists give the impression of being indifferent to technique. I can't be. The lesson I learnt from Turgenev was that books have to be made: a good chair doesn't collapse when you sit on it. He taught me, too, that the writing of novels is not a matter of doing one's own thing. One must look beyond oneself, and make the attempt at entering the minds of others. Each human being is unique, and to some extent mysterious. I want to solve the mystery of why people are like they are; I want to celebrate the uniqueness of my fellow creatures.

No E. Nesbit, no Beatrix Potter, no *Treasure Island*: mine was a deprived childhood. The literature in my early life consisted of comics, the magazines my mother and my aunts read, and adventure stories about boys who were strong, clean and decent. When I was ten, the miracle happened—I discovered Literature. My father read to me some chapters of *Nicholas Nickleby*; not long after, I was reading it for myself. I went to a grammar school, where I was encouraged to extend my limited knowledge of books by a kind, patient, understanding English master. He introduced me to Stevenson, Conan Doyle, and many other writers. Under his guidance, Shakespeare was from the very start a living force for me.

Which, of course, he still is. Reading his plays gives me the deepest pleasure I know. It's like saying a rose is a rose, but Shakespeare really doesn't have an equal in English. The first time I read *Antony and Cleopatra* I wept for joy at the incomparable beauty of its language. I shall never cease to find it anything but incredible that with three words, 'Husband, I come', Shakespeare can move one to the heart's core. This is the writing to live with, to aspire towards, to take into the bloodstream.

An obvious choice, but to say that I read the majority of Shakespeare's plays every year is to state nothing less than the truth. Not to read the inexhaustible is, quite simply, not to read. Keats knew this, and I can't say the knowledge did him much harm.

As a boy I was nicknamed 'Bleeding Macbeth' (the language was salty in the part of London I grew up in): I was proud to be so called. With a sense of determination I have never been able to muster since, I learnt all of *Hamlet* when I was thirteen or fourteen. I'm glad I did, as I'm also glad that—following the advice of one of the most civilized human beings I have been honoured to know—I learnt a poem every day from my thirteenth year to my twentieth. Oh God, this must strike a reader as being impossibly toffee-nosed, but it is, nevertheless, something I'm proud of having done. Those poems—by Donne, Herbert, Marvell, Keats—were living things and warm to me; they mattered. In Italy, children quote Dante and Manzoni from memory: the children I listened to weren't parrots, either; parrots aren't known to delight unashamedly in the fact that writers of genius can transform the most banal terms of everyday speech into a rare music.

I said at the beginning that I decided to become a writer after reading Turgenev. Well, I have to confess that I hardly read him now. As I get older it's the wild risk-takers who appeal to me most—Dostoyevsky, in particular. Only certain scenes in his books, but then what scenes they are! And those impossible, tortured, desperate creatures he creates: on first acquaintance, almost unbelievable, but on second, third, fourth so very much like our hidden selves. He is the supreme describer of that side of man which has to be suppressed, despite the preachings of R. D. Laing (many of whose ideas I would endorse) and the fashionable extremism of the cosily placed. Dostoyevsky's people are redeemed. This is not always the lot of people in the real world.

Dickens is my favourite risk-taker. I've never lost my love for his books: as with Shakespeare, I read him every year. One book in particular—*Great Expectations*. I'm constantly surprised and delighted by it—by Jaggers and his boots, and his hand-washing; by Miss Havisham (who I find totally credible); by Wemmick's two personalities; but most of all, by Pip and the love he learns to feel for Magwitch. No scene in an English novel affects me like the scene in which Pip assures the hunted, shackled man who was his benefactor that he will stay with him to the end. Pip's 'I will never stir from your side' is like Leontes' 'O, she's warm!'—a cry from the heart of a man who has found his soul.

Let me mention one other book: Svevo's *Confessions of Zeno*. I think this novel has influenced me more than any other. The death of Zeno's father, and Zeno's extraordinary behaviour at the death-bed—that scene will always haunt me with its truthfulness. It is the most unsettling comic novel I know of, and Zeno's battered dignity seems to me a wonderful conception—an everyday dignity, both tainted and ennobled by the ridiculous.

Finally, a list of the books and authors I most admire and always keep by me:

Jane Austen; *La Divina Commedia;* Conrad—particularly *The Secret Agent* and *Heart of Darkness; The Good Soldier; The Great Gatsby;* Eliot—everything before *Ash Wednesday*; John Clare; Hogg's *Confessions of a Justified Sinner*; Montale; Cavafy; *Dubliners* and *Ulysses*; Chekhov—stories *and* plays; Auden: *Collected Shorter Poems,* 1930–44; Simone Weil; Cole Porter's lyrics; Dorothy Parker; Ronald Firbank—especially *Vainglory* and *Pirelli*; *A Handful of Dust;* Isaac Babel; *Eggs, Beans and Crumpets;* Keats' *Letters*; Thomas Mann; Henry Green—*Loving* and *Caught*; Elizabeth Taylor's short stories...

DAVID BENEDICTUS

The Conjuror's Frayed Hem

I should like to take you back, but I forget the way. So much, of which I remember so little. Phrases, images, pictures, irrelevancies. I just remember *Just William* and the rough boys and his mother and her tea-parties, but vividly I recall the red binding which turned the bath water a sinister pink. And the huge book of fairy stories, too heavy almost to lift, with the beautiful pictures printed on shiny paper—I think they must have been Arthur Rackhams, for they inhabited the erotic world of faery all right, and infected all our dreams. One picture, was it the frontispiece?, a fairy on a swing, ah!, but what I mean to say is ... ah!

Otherwise, shreds, alas, and tatters. *The Baron de Bong and the Chief of Police and the Dog from Next Door, and the Nephew and Niece*—is that right? It doesn't sound right. There was such joy in the assonance, and such funny pictures—a balloon came into it somewhere, sailing serenely over toy villages with heads craning up to see—and the rhymed narrative lying doggo beneath them.

Ah yes, now it starts to seep back through the porous cells of my spongy brain. *Fattipuffs and Thinnifers*—that *was* a favourite. Two worlds, contradictory and complementary, in one of which everything was fat—the bushy-topped trees, the doughnuts, the waddling dogs, the bulging architectures, all bosses and buttresses, the elephants, the puffy clouds; and in the other everything was thin—conifers, bananas, borzois, crenellated, perpendicular, spired churches, giraffes, cirrus, herring-bone skies. A metaphor that could be indefinitely continued at home (my sister was bonny, and I skin and bone). One could still play it, I suppose, with adult hindsight. Christians and Ted-led, milk-fed Tories and Russians and the Big Bomb and the Queen are Fattipuffs, while Jeremy Thorpe —and the Liberals generally with one notable exception—and Brahmins and the third world and SAM missiles and Prince Philip are Thinnifers. The feminine and masculine principles perhaps. But I'm no Thinnifer now.

Ah, and adventures! Yes, gosh, wow! That awful witch, what *was* her name, not Gooliguts, nor Golgotha, but something like that, in *King Solomon's Mines*, crushed to death—oh horror, oh joy!—in the sliding rocks, and *She*, the eternal, mysterious female, beautiful and her bosoms actually visible through the halo of transcendence with which the Victorian artist had thought fit to encircle her. How they hunted her down, until she was consumed in the flames, and turned into a hag, just like Mrs—but, no, she might still be alive, having somehow escaped the sliding rocks of the passing years.

But *adventures*, oh yes, golly, wizard, *Castle of Adventure, Island of Adventure, Five Do This, Five Do That, Five Go On A Treasure Hunt, The Thirty-Nine Steps,* and *Bunkle and Belinda* written by Philip Swift's Mum, so that, although Philip was terrified of flies—of *flies*!—we forgave him, bathed as he was in the surrogate glamour of a Bunkling Son of a Bunkling Mum. And Biggles in his goggles, notching swastikas on the side of his Sopwith Camel. And when all the tattered Biggles were out of the school library (which was usually), one could cast a sly glance at the Worralls—though of course *she* was only a girl, notwithstanding she behaved like a chap. And the Saint could always be depended upon, showing no mercy, for instance, to the unacceptable face of capitalism—a greedy truck-hire man who overworked his drivers, keeping them on the road until they fell asleep, but the Saint strapped him to a seat, and projected a winding road in front of him, put his hands on the steering wheel, and, and—crikey!—flogged him with a belt every time he hit the kerb, ho ho! All right too. Smashing, and serve him right. A leaf out of Bulldog Drummond's book, and old Hugh didn't lag far behind, because he had a penchant for dipping people in acid, and paying in kind those Bolshevik toadies of the great Carl Peterson (ah, if he could have joined forces with Moriarty!) when they tortured dear old absent-minded professors into revealing state secrets and priceless inventions which they needed for their own nefarious ends. And when Carl Peterson met his death in that beautifully appointed dirigible, one still had Irma, who 'handled her Hispano Suiza like a sensitive animal', such a poetic phrase, and one which has lingered with me through thick and thin though I've never met a girl who owned one, and, if I had, I should have wanted to do the driving. Like a sensitive animal, of course.

And Irma was just one of a long line of sexy spectres. Remember the Marsh King's Daughter, rising naked and unashamed in that unforgettable wood-cut, and She (q.v.) and the two skinny little girls in *The Wind Round the Moon*, one standing on the other's shoulders as they hid their bundle of clothes in a hollow tree. Two lovely bums, four dimples; obsessed? You bet!

If course there were disasters. Why did they keep on throwing Harrison Ainsworth at me? Who was Harrison Ainsworth? Could anyone read him? Apart from anything else the volumes *looked* so boring, not just without pictures or conversations but with tiny print so tedious to decipher, even under the sheets. (Ah yes, we covered the torch-head with a stretched handkerchief, and when our eyes could no longer stand the strain put the torch into our mouths so that our cheeks became red and translucent.) And those *awful* Arthur

Ransomes. Such wet children, sailing about the place, being so nice and pi and knowing everything about everything, and all that tiresome old nature. They were so ... wet! Rather than that I'd 'borrow' Janice's Angela Brazils and skim through *The Naughtiest Girl is a Monitor,* which was just like a boys' school story, only they tended to capture German parachutists and go moony over poetry, while the boys were fighting for the honour of the school in pads and flannels (the girls did that sometimes too). Let's see, there was Ian Hay and P. G.Wodehouse, *Stalky and Co.* and *Vice Versa* (I loved that one) and *Tom Brown's Schooldays* and the *Jeremy* stories by Hugh Walpole, which were, well, a bit weird somehow. Disturbing echoes of an adult world that we didn't entirely welcome, although we knew we had left those fairies way behind.

'Oh where are the other girls and boys?
And why have you brought me children's toys?'

I read everything. Didn't care. Dickens, *Pooh,* Linklater, *Babar, San Michele, A Warning to Wantons, The Wooden Horse,* Jane Austen, Schoolboy Annuals, *Lost Horizon,* Lewis Carroll, *Gulliver,* Enid Blyton's weekly *Sunny Stories,* the *Eagle,* of course, with the ineffable Dan Dare and Harris Tweed—and to this day I'm confused as to whether he was an advertisement or a feature, but hilarious he unquestionably was—and *Beano,* and the *Life of Danny Kaye,* and, oh anything, even if it was *wet.*

And of all those words, which were in the air I breathed, which were absorbed through my pores, what do I most vividly retain? So little, so pitiably little. A bear being dragged upstairs by a boy? A looking-glass with unusual properties? The Saint's cool elegance or Uriah Heep's reptilian unctuousness? Becky Sharp or the Cranford ladies or those green-headed huge-domed things with the ray guns? No, none of these, particularly, but ...

The curious lobster stranded inland with the relentless sun drying his beautiful shell. Oh lord. Oh lord. If he doesn't get back to the river quickly, quickly, he'll be all dried up and deaded. Oh hurry, lobster. Oh something happen; quickleeeee!

Am I drying up? Can't I get back to the salty waters which will salve and refresh me and make me again what I was? Books were magic, they were urgent, their words had hooks on them that grabbed you, but now I write them and, forgive me, review them, it's as though I'd crawled behind the conjuror's table and seen the rabbit waiting there with red astonished eyes for his startling appearance out of thin air; seen too the frayed hem of the conjuror's jacket, the cigarette hastily jabbed out before the performance and still smoking, the spare wand.

I didn't want to see all that. Why did they let me? Why didn't the conjuror insist that I stay where I was, as mystified as all the rest at the wonderful magic which came after the jellies. Magic? Only a box of tricks!

MELVYN BRAGG

A Self-Portrait in Books

First I drew up an instant list from memory. Then I set off round the bookshelves and had scarcely moved before I was in possession of an armful of favourites which needed re-reading urgently. I reverted to the original list—random, incomplete and obvious it most certainly is; but at least it's manageable.

The books which came to mind were in every case books to which I had been addicted. Authors I have followed through to their last short story, neglecting no clue in the public library or the publisher's fly-leaf; books I'd finished and immediately re-started; characters I'd imitated; words I'd remembered; incidents I'd tested against plausibility and credibility again and again—above all, work to which I can return in my mind whenever I want and, equally important, work which itself returns to mind without my wanting or not wanting. To begin at the beginning—

Hymns and comics: or rather, hymns and psalms and comic papers and radio comedians. In exuberant or sentimental moods I am doused in early childhood and break the surface full of Wesley, the greatest hymn-writer of any age or Wilson, the divine athlete from the *Wizard*. Suitably primed I can, modestly I lay this claim, out-last anyone on the *Ancient and Modern*, the shorter psalms, parts of the litany, feast-day gospels and epistles and occasional anthems of high sentence and many dotted semiquavers. Though I'm an Anglican, this bent of mind helped me, later, to wallow in James Joyce's Catholic epiphanies and rhapsodies, for example, while the prayer-book prose and Jacobean rhythm made the Elizabethans, and others, accessible and redolent. The rhyme schemes in the hymnal are dull and the tunes are rarely collectors' items, but together the pulse has, I believe, operated as a bass line on which my enjoyment of poetry has been reared.

If the Church gave the word, comics gave the deed. Each week I was left dangling by a fingernail, part of me in some sort of real pain at the effort to survive until the next instalment from the *Wizard, Rover, Hotspur* or *Adventure*. Dickens, later, another addiction, was something of a dour old naturalist after the fantastical plots in the comics; his famous chapter-endings mere cracks in the story-line. I'd been used to seven-day suspense across a ravine (bottomless—invariably); moreover, his 'heroes', the often criticized instruments of innocence which sew the novels together, were raw and hunky humans after the ethereal presences of Wilson or the Wonder Man, or that sexless obsessive ageless freak whose total existence rested in his right boot—I refer, as the cognoscenti need no telling, to Cannonball Kid; or Limp-Along Leslie (the Calvinist version); or Nick Smith (for fathers as well as sons). And then there was the Tough of the Track—Alf Tupper—ah well! No real villains though; Quilp broke new ground.

The *Dandy* and *Beano* had been all right, but for laughs it was the wireless and we sat around as in an advertisement while the jokes came out of the second-hand radio on a sideboard and we all ssshhd each other to catch the next line: Ted Kavanagh, Frank Muir and Dennis Norden, generally, wrote the script. The first time I remember laughing aloud at jokes in books was with P. G. Wodehouse and later *Lucky Jim*.

The real laughs came from the town gossip—the stories of

the 'characters'—and for most people in a working-class environment such as mine (and for all I know, in other environments) this joking was the chief 'book'. When I came to read *Under Milk Wood*, it was like our street in sing-song English—even a social documentary; *Our Town*, too, was instantly recognizable and far and away the most popular school play. (American accents were no problem whatsoever after three changes of western a week—but that's another story.) For thirteen years now I've attempted to write fiction as funny and unexpected as the local chat and failed for fear of caricature, lack of self-confidence and a lack of the talent. Perhaps the comic spirit will descend one day if only I could stop looking up.

Pre-teens was a mush. Public school stories wherein impossibly reticent and able young men executed enviable deeds in white flannels or the teeth of adversity. Oh *Fifth Form at St Dominic's*, where are you now? And how, but through the insidious nectar of imagination, could such flat prose recording the banal accomplishments of over-privileged embryo-imperialists have such shameless effects on the brain of a slitter's son in no-nonsense Cumberland? There never seemed to be a grammar-school hero—let alone an unheroic and home-loving grammar-school fantasist.

Besides this there were those inflammatory documents, the *People* and the *News of the World*, which in puberty excited my fears—as you might say, gentle reader, so much that I did not know whether I was about to murder, rape, betray my country or change sex—'She was a normal healthy sailor until last March.' Perhaps readers of these literary essays cannot envisage a world which comes to you on Sundays only (after church) and through those two papers. Believing every word the worlds of Grimm and of Sodom and Gomorrah seemed as Disneyland compared with Soho of the early 'fifties. Through it all I held on to the *Women's Illustrated*, my mother's book, and, in the face of overwhelming evidence, odds and inclination, believed that somewhere, out there, was a world of young, fair-haired shy doctors, and lithe, tanned, mischievous nurses. Emancipated biology arrived just in time.

In adolescence came voracity and I could pick out print at five hundred yards. I attempted to read my way through the school library, I remember that, but only at the end of dreams do I remember the books themselves and then, like some monster from the Loch Ness of one's consciousness, up swims a chapter or a page of dialogue or description from—who was it? Reade? Scott? Walpole? Carlyle? Many others?

If there was one particular strand in the two or three years before University, then it was American fiction. Steinbeck above all. Aldous Huxley gave me a whiff of intellectual grapeshot, much thanks; Dostoyevsky took over from the missing growth of the Church and squeezed what I could still call my soul; all those books in the school library filled in the gaps. Gide crept tentatively into a quiet corner and discreetly proposed an *acte gratuite*; Maugham was rapidly read for tips on what to do in the Far East with passion and tradition—and so on. But it was out West we went; in the trail of the pioneers, across the deserts to California we were lured and there, East of Eden, were the Grapes of Wrath. On the way, Fitzgerald had been gobbled up to be reserved for a later date; Hemingway met for a showdown at the corral (unfair to *For Whom The Bell Tolls*, which still electrifies me at the memory of the shared sleeping bag, and *The Sun Also Rises,* where they spoke and acted like men but also, no flip side, 'real' men) and the other Americans had been encountered—contemporaries, that is—Hawthorne, Twain, even Melville had to wait. But Steinbeck was king and of his progeny *Cannery Row* was my addiction. In one way it was the apotheosis of my childhood, youth and adolescence. The place was, quite clearly, very like Wigton, Cumberland. The boyos, *our* very own unemployed: their truths, our truths, the language, Old Testament, with the occasional up-to-date Song of Solomon. Whorehouses! Chinamen who tried to cheat at chess! Liquor! Sloth! And —like in the comics, effortless superiority, innate nobility.

Most of all, a real America, a place, there, undeniable. My first attempts at fiction were to re-write *Cannery Row*, setting it in my own town.

Before going to University where books made a take-over bid, thwarted by life only after a struggle, I want to mention several books now clamouring to get out and repeat themselves on this occasion—everyone should have prizes. One a year, say, from 11 to 17. *John Halifax, Gentleman; Kidnapped; Pilgrim's Progress; Nigger of the Narcissus*—neither enjoyed nor fully understood but held on to for some other reason; Trevelyan's social history; Guy de Maupassant's stories; and Collingwood's *Idea of History*. The last, pressed on me by the history teacher, gave me a taste for a sort of writing which I could never fully comprehend and has since let me brood in tolerable bewilderment right up to Strawson, Chomsky and Wittgenstein.

Also there developed an affection for poetry which seems to keep growing. Then it was founded on the set books. On Chaucer, which I could accept the more easily because the English teacher had the idea of reading it in the Cumbrian dialect (which I spoke: not as a preservative gesture but as a matter of fact) and the lines fitted beautifully into the Nordic grooves. On Keats, whose epithets tickled my fancy and my skin. And finally on Wordsworth, whom I liked then chiefly, perhaps, for his local worth but also for his neurotic and philosophical centre which glows and fades but never dies away. Wordsworth has become an uncle now—and the sensation of literally and sensorially covering the same ground as he did (minnows and whales, of course) continues as a preoccupation. I'd like to write a poem beginning 'Listen, W.W. ...'.

Oxford was to change a lot, but before that I read books which in terms of the dreadful 'influence' could have had an effect. I hope so. I've had to put up with a bit on this subject. Critics by the dozen have compared me with D. H. Lawrence and Thomas Hardy particularly: and then other critics have taken the trouble to denounce me for presuming I was anything *like* Thomas Hardy or D. H. Lawrence. I'd read *Sons and Lovers* at school, I remember, and been very moved by it but for some reason I didn't go on and did not get into Lawrence until towards the end of University, when I found his poems, and from then on tracked down everything with increasing pleasure and awe which still continues. Hardy I can't remember reading until my twenties, but there again I had to go through everything and still turn to him, particularly the poems and *Return of the Native*. No, the road to Damascus book for me was *Buddenbrooks*. I read it five times on the trot—or rather on my stomach beside the tennis courts in the summer before University, looking up now and then to watch the swirl of pleated skirts. Instantly I wanted to write a three-generation novel about my own class—as compact with incident and culture as this book—in every way as weighty. I read more of Mann. *Tonio Kröger* probably set my mind on being a writer—and gave me the idea that one had to be leisured, dedicated, detached and somehow prepared to take unnameable personal risks.

I wonder why no one has done an anthology like this before? It's like going back to your home town after you've been away a year or so and finding to your amazement that people are pleased to see you. And you them.

Oxford was a welter of words and so to be brief the most important thing for me, I guess, was that I managed to drag myself into the first quarter of the twentieth century. Ezra Pound's essays stunned me. *His* reading lists—remember them? I felt (stupidly) illiterate. Eliot, Joyce and David Jones; John Cowper Powys, whom I stumbled on then—his *In Defence of Sensuality*—and stuck to, through *Wolf Solent* to *A Glastonbury Romance*; Sartre and Kafka and Camus—of course the Sisyphus Generation; the Beats came in and then there was the night I read *Tropic of Cancer* and spoke like Henry Miller for days afterwards. I read a lot of plays for some reason—Tennessee Williams complete one weekend; O'Neill;

Lorca; Brecht. One way or another I came up against the Moderns and crept nearer the Contemporaries.

There was something else at Oxford which continued for about ten years afterwards and has now lapsed, regrettably I sometimes think, other times I'm relieved. And that was a modest desire to be an encyclopaedia. I tried to slog through Marx and Darwin, Francis Bacon's *Essays*, Lao Tzu, Bullfinch's *Mythology*, Einstein, *The Universal Biography*, Julian Huxley's potboilers (sweathouses for me), H. G. Wells's *World History, The Dawn of Civilization*, Lenin, Freud, Nietzsche, Windt, Vasari —there had to be a limit and I hoped to find it. *Herzog* came in like an echo—'implosive' was a fashionable word at about that time and Mr Bellow's hero certainly imploded in me.

As I say, this has slipped away although corners are stacked high with paperback introductions, selections, anthologies, condensations and even the complete works. A few months ago, though, I was doing a film on Hardy and went to Dorchester, where I looked through his notebooks. There, aged forty-seven, he is still making reading lists, proud of every poem read, even noting down a sonnet at the year's end, full of worth. It was chastening all right.

Since University then there has been so much that even the space offered by this encouraging editor could not cope. It would be cowardly to blanch before the obvious or the mighty: Shakespeare, Dickens, George Eliot (especially *Felix Holt*), Fielding, Lawrence, Conrad, Mann, Twain, Jane Austen *et al.* The greater and lesser traditions are always around and generally in any year I return to re-read some of each. To that list I suppose I'd add Faulkner, Balzac, Svevo, Joyce; tentatively Proust. (Tentative because I've only managed three volumes so far—re-read though, three times), Ibsen, Kirkegaard and all the Russians. The one country which I felt I discovered for myself and held to myself was Russia. From Pushkin to Solzhenitsyn, but most of all Tolstoy and Chekhov and most of all *Anna Karenina* and *The Seagull*. I read Chekhov's short stories often and Tolstoy's *The Cossacks* always puts me right.

Those apart, though, and passing over the manias for Agatha Christie, Simenon and Chandler; for political biography and Runciman and the works of T. W. Carrick—here are a few authors on whom I can at this moment get a useful fix.

Graham Greene—pounded through in about a fortnight seven or eight years ago when his skill enthralled me. My books I thought, and at the time regretted it, were plotless, plotless and above all plotless and here was a man who could turn them out like perfect ball bearings. Sylvia Plath for her accuracy in simile and in describing pain. Evelyn Waugh, who took me by surprise, by the throat in the trilogy, and whose life and works (which became one; those diaries were a posthumous novel—perfected to bamboozle) are like nothing else—he grows year by year. Mailer, too, whose *Advertisements for Myself* made me try things I would never have dared or dreamed of; the fact that I fell flat on my face was not important. Scott Fitzgerald; Malamud's stories; Borges's ideas; Edmund Wilson's achieved encyclopaedia; Malraux; Beckett in small sips; enough.

One last book—*Moby Dick*. A new world.

As a postscript I acknowledge that I have missed out many favourites and all my contemporaries but here one reads with a different eye. Of the generation ahead of me in England, another time; of my own well, forty years on, when the dust settles.

BRIGID BROPHY

My personality can scarcely have been formed before I found it an intolerable one to live with. Left to myself, I fled my self. Either I committed temporary suicide by total immersion in a book or I became an alternative self.

This is the paradox (which I have tried to explore in a novel named *In Transit*) of the literary imagination. For an imaginative writer, 'self-expression' consists of expressing selves, experiences and atmospheres of mind that are, precisely, *not* his. And for a compulsive reader self-gratification is achieved by renouncing the self, its sense-data and satisfactions, in favour of one of the alternative experiences created by writers.

By the age of three, the point where my more-or-less continuous memory begins, I was already an addicted reader. I still crave daily immersion in experience other than my own (it needn't be more pleasant, exciting or illuminating—merely other) and I still fall into books as though into catalepsy. I have learnt, however, to keep a particle of my proper self alive: enough to admire the author's design as I speed through it, and enough to notice whether my personal experience tallies with or contradicts my experience inside the book. As a child I exercised no such criticism, external or internal. I purely experienced books.

In consequence, I was unable to reply to the questions adults asked me about the books I read. 'Do you like it?' was to me meaningless. I didn't read in order to like or dislike the experience: but in order to *have* it. To me a book was a Popish cosmos, in which whatever was right.

My failure to answer the other regular question, 'What's it about?', must have made me seem an exceptionally stupid child. The truth was that I couldn't remember. My reading self and my proper self were to such an extent alternatives, usurpers of each other, that they didn't share a memory. When I shut a book I totally forgot its content. But I remembered it totally the instant I opened the book again.

Indeed, the phenomenon of split personality, where a person is both X and Y and can recall X's past only when he is X and Y's only when he is Y, seems to me merely an exaggeration of the normal imaginative state. It is strange in being watertight, whereas my literary amnesia was a one-way transaction (I could be recalled from my book to my proper self, but then my proper self could not recall what I had just been reading) and strange in the specificness of its compulsion. The victim of split personality is given no choice whether to be X or Y today. The literary addict has some leeway about when and which, but he too is under an inescapable compulsion to enter *some* alternative experience.

As a child I was, when not drowned in a book, a split or a positively frayed personality, free only to choose which of my countless alternative selves I would be. My regular repertory was enlarged by personae borrowed from my reading, but my literary amnesia forced me to be largely self-reliant in matters of incident. Indeed, I was committing a genuine proto-literary act. In technique and, occasionally, material, my impersonations resembled daydreams, but from the moment (which came later) when I perfected the habit of daydreaming I was conscious of the difference. The daydreams promoted the self. The impersonations replaced it. I valued my daydreams for making me, in fantasy, bigger and better. The impersonations merely and neutrally made me other. They were hypotheses of alternative experiences—that is, embryo works of fiction, since a fiction is a hypothesis, though the tests it is subject to are different from those that apply to the scientific kind.

Between reading and proto-writing I was shuttlecocked by a tension between my parents. It was a tension compatible with their being very happy together and giving me a happy childhood—as well as a head start, over most people born into the pre-war suburbs, in the subject of sex equality. My father was a writer, my mother a teacher (and many other things; she is too adventurous to settle to or for one job). Consequently, in our household it was the father who stayed at home and the mother who went out to work—and who indeed became furious with frustration if she ever had to spend a day in.

I think it was my mother who taught me to read (I have no memory of learning), probably so that I should be able to amuse myself and thus let her out of the house. But it was my father who provided the books. He was a prolific reviewer, who never sold a review copy, and an autodidact specialist (in Shakespeare, military history, eighteenth-century Ireland and etymology), who copiously bought second-hand books on his special subjects and any other that took his fancy.

From the start I had the run of the books. By the time I was six, my mother was headmistress of a prep school and we had moved into the school house, a hideous pebble-dashed caricature of, at once, château and chalet. To my father the move meant more and larger rooms to fill with books. To me it meant having the run not only of his multiplying books but, out of school hours, of the school library.

My mother, however, though she was not officially against literature and had even (one of her odd jobs) published a novel herself, deplored the books. They meant to her dust and untidiness, which she hated not because she was domesticated but because she wasn't—and yet couldn't free herself from the moral obligations of domesticity. She wished the books absent. But since they were there, she believed she must clean them.

Twice a year, red in the face with anger at being indoors when she might have been taking a twenty-mile bicycle ride, she put a scarf over her hair, tucked her skirt inside her pink knickers (less a practical gesture, I now think, than a left-over of little-girl rudeness), stamped up a ladder and banged the books' heads together.

Perhaps because she associated them with dust, she took to telling me to stop reading books and get out into the fresh air. Perhaps because she feared that, in my precocity, I too would soon start filling rooms with books, she took to adding that I would have plenty of time for reading grown-up books when I was grown-up and should meanwhile be playing with someone my own age.

I obeyed. I went out into the garden (which, since it was also the school playground, was large) and marched about being —in blank verse and sixteenth-century idiom and at the top of my voice—several other people.

I made no objection to other children joining in, though I judged their companionableness strictly by their powers of improvising dialogue.

My first disappointment (which probably turned me from a poet into a prose-writer) was that none of them was willing to improvise in blank verse. My technique, however, remained that of drama, though prose drama. Indeed, I presently became a dramatist. An elderly lady who lived in the next road appointed herself my impresario and me her dramatist-in-residence. I was ten and my sixth play was in production when the war began and my family moved—and no doubt it was despair of ever finding so generous a niche again that made me begin my professional career as an author of books rather than plays.

Of my early literary experience all that remains intact is my shunning of my self. I now have one, of course, and am glad of it in close relationships, though even there I adopt verbal devices that turn me from a first into a third person. I am uneasy in any social setting that exposes a self that is neither reader nor writer—at any gathering, in short, where the proprieties forbid me either to vanish into someone else's book or to concentrate on the next paragraph of my own.

When I abandoned spoken words as my medium and adopted words designed to be read, I lost command of the quasi-Shakespearean rhythm that was second nature to me and tried to learn a quasi-Shavian one. Shaw's prefaces were among the works I read and re-read, forgot and re-forgot, throughout my childhood. I have only to open them now to remember that I have known most of most of them by heart most of my life—and to re-recognize that Shaw's expository prose is the most flexible yet robust literary instrument ever devised, as comely and as apt to all literary purposes as the architectural idiom of Dublin is comely and apt to all social purposes.

In becoming literate, I sacrificed my native fluency. I now halt in conversation; I would sooner send a card than make a telephone call; I listen more happily to music if I have the score in front of me; I can't learn a name let alone a language by 'direct method'. (Naturally what I read at Oxford consisted of two dead—that is, written—languages. Naturally I don't like meeting people extempore when I fail to register Derek Smith until I am sure he in fact is so and not Deryk Smythe.)

Yet for all that I am so deep-layered in the sophistications of literacy that a misplaced comma can make me blush, I am a little flimsy about the foundations. My tutor said: 'I don't see why, if you can spell in English, you can't spell in Greek.' I was ashamed to explain. Much earlier my mother had said: 'I don't see how a person who reads as many books as you do can avoid having the spelling of a word imprinted on her mind.'

I don't see how, either, but I have avoided it. Consciously at least, I'm not in rebellion against the anarchy of English spelling. Perhaps because I seem myself to have learnt too painlessly to remember, I don't sympathize with Shaw's belief that children waste time and effort in learning to read English. (I'm not convinced children learn quicker in phonetically spelt languages like Italian or end up more literate.) I wish Shaw had put his thought and money into reforming not English spelling but musical notation (whose unreformed state doesn't seem to have bothered him in the least). The fact that the eye doesn't see, as on a graph, what the ear hears—that the distance from a line to the adjoining space sometimes represents a tone and at other times a semi-tone—is as lunatic as if a map-maker made part of his map on a 1:200 scale and another part on 1:400. (Reform itself is easy, but not succinct reform. Several of the systems I have devised work perfectly except that they would require a full orchestral score to be five foot high.)

Not being in rebellion on this matter, I try to conform to standard orthography. I can't, however, remember the spelling even of commonplace words I use every day. I have to look them up every day. And looking them up takes me longer than it should. If our language spoke, as many do, of analphabetism rather than illiteracy, I should find myself on the brink of it. I do in fact know the order of the English alphabet (and of the Greek; I even know, in correct order, the Italian names of the letters). But I am not at home in it, and second-stage alphabetical order exposes my shakiness. I waste hours, as I try to consult the dictionary, in disputing whether *mn-* comes before or after *mo-*.

Perhaps I am in rebellion against the order of the alphabet, which is so arbitrary as to constitute anti-order. Or perhaps whoever taught me to read omitted to teach me the alphabet. I can't, of course, remember.

Students of the psychopathology of everyday life (and of etymology or Greek) will have noticed that both my statement that I can't remember whether I was taught and my accusatory suspicion that I wasn't are incarnate in the examples it came to my encrustedly literate mind to give of second-stage alphabetical order.

DAVID CAUTE

There were no brothers or sisters and there was no television. Nor was there much continuity in childhood friendships; the war kept us on the move, my mother and I, with our radio and our books. She told me often that a bomb had fallen on a London warehouse, destroying some furniture and a rich library of books. The books obviously mattered to her most, I was completely exposed to her values, and I don't regret it. From an early age I was in awe of books, the neat rows of print, the publisher's mark and date, the yellowing, brittle paper of first editions, the incomparable glory of authorship. The mystical power of the artist, the conjuror, hypnotized me; I desired then (as now) merely to give edification and pleasure to a whole nation of helplessly addicted admirers.

Yet I read as a child reads, haphazardly, eclectically, picking my nose and begging for sweets. The child is the ideal reader, innocently scavenging, naked to entertainment, uncontaminated by a sense of cultural obligation. (In this respect the children of the twentieth century are more fortunate than their nineteenth-century forebears—one recoils in horror from the literary and academic precocity imposed on a Mill or a Flaubert, much as one might like to be a Mill or a Flaubert. And I believe, also, that we, the last generation to grow up in the absence of television, enjoy a certain advantage over our children: simply because the eye is the most inquisitive of the human sense organs, we learned through books and radio to *translate* images from one medium to another, to visualize, in private metamorphosis' scenes, faces and confrontations which today are served up ready-made—and hence pale—by the round-the-clock electronic barbarism. There is evidence to show that the capacity to *imagine* is intimately linked to the capacity to 'work', in the sense of generating a dynamic relationship with one's environment.)

I would prefer to confine my recollection s to some books read during childhood and adolescence. I have to admit that reading is ideally an amateur pursuit. As soon as it becomes an integral function of one's professional life, that vital sense of a unique occasion particular to each good book is eroded by a thick-skinned pragmatism. Books become instruments to be raped in quick succession, to be gutted for the information, point of view or style they yield; gone is the capacity to brood and dream with a book on one's lap, with today gently ebbing into tomorrow. For children books secrete a whole world; they offer experiences to be re-told, re-created, and re-read. They are not to be tamed by the categories of 'naturalism', 'expressionism' or 'socialist realism', nor are they to be tormented into the analytical patterns of 'comparative literature'. The deadly impact of 'criticism' has not yet begun to numb responsiveness. With books, as with love affairs, the loss of innocence is a catastrophe.

It is not always easy to remember when, exactly, one read particular books. Occasionally (I now discover) I inscribed a date under my name on the fly-page, but this proprietorial gesture may well have been that of the absentee landlord. Many novels, judged 'suitable' by culture-bound relatives, prove too difficult on the first encounter—the wordy preliminary descriptions favoured by Sir Walter Scott were notably exasperating. I can be fairly sure that *Dr Doolittle, Winnie The Pooh, Rupert Bear, Babar the Elephant,* and the versified visits of A. A. Milne's Christopher Robin to Buckingham Palace figured among my earliest favourites, along with the Walrus and the Carpenter, the toeless Pobble, and the Pied Piper. But such characters as Long John Silver, Gulliver or Robin Hood are served up in so many versions of varying simplicity that it is inpossible to recall when they first entered the scene.

Though reading ability advances rapidly during the years of classic childhood (6 to 12), I find it easier to treat the period as a unit. Once the first, wide-eyed encounters with fantasy had been absorbed, I soon developed a taste for richness of social detail, vivid characterization, an intricate and enthralling story, and, if possible, a historical setting. Pathos, too, was important: I was very keen to shed tears, and so intense was my capacity for empathy that self-pity invariably resulted. It was I, not little Mowgli, who fought an ingenious battle for survival in the jungle, befriended by the black panther Bagheera and menaced by the sinister tiger Shere Khan; it was I, not Oliver Twist, who held up his bowl for more; and by the time I had finished *David Copperfield* I regarded myself as so tragic and heroic a little man as to be virtually unapproachable. The addiction to pathos was to endure, wrapping a suppurating sludge of sentimentality round Walpole's *Judith Paris,* Margaret Mitchell's *Gone With the Wind*, Richard Llewellyn's *How Green Was My Valley,* and James Hilton's *Lost Horizon.*

Of course, not all of these are bad books, I don't mean to disparage them. My solemn, but justified, concern for the plight of the poor tended to blur the lines of discrimination, and I don't blame myself for having regarded *Germinal* and *Anna of the Five Towns* as the Greatest Books Ever Written. (I wrote them, incidentally—if literature was a sacrament, I was never less than its high priest.)

In the child-reader one notices a delicious tension: he yearns to grow up in a hurry, at the same time rejoicing in the exuberant crimes of childhood. Books both reflect and exacerbate the contradiction. The riveting thing about E. Nesbit's *The Railway Children* or Arthur Ransome's *Swallows and Amazons* adventures, or *The Pioneer Twins*, or *Emile and the Detectives*, is the gallant assumption of adult responsibilities (and capacities) by little people. Gosh! On the other hand, Billy Bunter and Richmal Crompton's iconoclastic William provide a therapeutic validation of the child's licensed access to every (relevant) deadly sin. And then there are the frightening books for and about children which some parents believe create traumas and other parents insist release traumas; but if *Alice* is often considered a book for adults in terms of literary appreciation, I would suggest that *Tom Brown's Schooldays* should be reserved only for those children likely to thrive on an encounter with the Holocaust. I have seen my own eight-year-old son gloatingly await the imminent bacteriological extinction of mankind in *Dr Who*, then scuttle into the kitchen as soon as the televised Tom Brown is confronted by the vicious prefect with the words, 'Ah, Brown ... '.

History, as I have said, exerted a terrific fascination. I loved the past, particularly the Middle Ages, the world of villeins and serfs, of burghers and craft guilds, of fallow fields and tithes. I suppose I did enjoy historical 'westerns' in the vein of Dumas (*The Count of Monte Cristo* was really smashing) or of Anthony Hope's Ruritanian romances (*Rupert of Hentzau*, etc.), but they were as nothing compared to Helen Waddell's *Peter Abelard*, the novels of Alfred Duggan, and—later—, Lion Feuchtwanger's *Jew Süss*. It was at an early age that I read G. M. Trevelyan's *English Social History* and the Quennells' marvellous *Everyday Life in England*, followed not long afterwards by Pepys and Chaucer, neither of whom I understood exactly but both of whom precipitated me into a fever of scribbling. *Tom Jones* worked the same trick.

For me this scribbling remains the umbilical cord—the convulsive leap from chair to table; the shameless plagiarism; the euphoric initial aspirations and the subsequent whimpering evaporation of inspiration, so that one Great Novel after another terminated in mid-sentence, usually on the second page. My passion then, as now, was for succulent, fat, hard-covered notebooks, hundreds of virgin-white, feint-ruled pages awaiting the inroads of my mock-tortoiseshell fountain pen. The parental indisposition to buy me new notebooks in a climate of austerity and in the face of my oft-proven propensity merely to spoil previous ones was only rarely shaken by my pleas for professional working conditions. It was abundantly clear to me that the real novels I read stretched from cover to cover, and were not tagged on to the end of earlier abortive efforts whose failure could obviously be ascribed to the fact that the author was then an immature nine rather than a uniquely gifted nine-and-a-half.

A true novelist was someone who could fill up all the pages, who could sustain a story, chapter after chapter, twisting, turning, grafting on new scenes, deepening the plot, thinking up something new to happen ... to the end. How I longed to be able to write, in good conscience, THE END. Alas, the first novel I completed was also the first I published, and that did not occur until I was a uniquely gifted twenty-and-a-half. A dream was taken from me: to write like Dickens at the age of eleven, and to have the whole world gape in awe and amazement. When I first heard Daisy Ashford's *The Young Visiters* serialized on the radio, I was possessed by joy and envy, with the latter emotion rapidly gaining the ascendant. And, yah, I bet it was J. M. Barrie or someone else who really wrote it.

I entered a John Buchan phase, read them all, wrote quite a few of them, in embryo. The sort of novels I really appreciated about the age of twelve were those in the English social-realist vein, Bennett and Galsworthy—no book has ever given me more pleasure than *The Forsyte Saga*. Sinclair Lewis's *Babbitt* and *Dodsworth* were also winners, and I had a taste for the seedy-shuffling-genteel world of the petty bourgeoisie as portrayed in Wells's *Mr Polly*, Dickens's *Pickwick Papers*, and Priestley's *Angel Pavement*. I liked funny books too: James Thurber, Stephen Leacock's *Literary Lapses*, etc., Jerome's

Three Men in a Boat, Wodehouse's *Jeeves*, and I was always a candidate for a good adventure- or war-story, whether *The Scarlet Pimpernel, Biggles,* Rider Haggard, Conan Doyle or the emerging Second World War stories like R. C. Rivaz's *Tail Gunner,* Deneys Reitz's *Commando, The Wooden Horse* and—now into adolescence and suddenly prey to exaggerated sexual emotion—Monsarrat's *The Cruel Sea.*

The radio was enormously important to me; it would be artificial to separate it from the experience of books, since both media fuelled the same fire, and I wrote just about as many one-minute radio plays as I did one-page novels. The best of radio, of course, carried no literary consequence, though almost anything can bake a yeasty imagination: *Toy Town* (years later the great Norman Shelley took a part in a radio play of mine and he was obviously touched by my expressions of awe and gratitude because no one honours those radio actors who give so much to so many, the knighthoods are all reserved for the glamour boys of the stage); *Dick Barton;* Tommy Handley; Frankie Howerd; the Goons. But, because I had practically no access to the legitimate theatre, my most formative experiences of performed drama were associated with radio, with James Forsyth's *The Nameless One of Europe* (a work of genius), with Henry Reed's *Streets of Pompeii*, with radio adaptations of Gabriel Marcel and Jean Anouilh, and with countless craftsmanlike Saturday evening plays whose titles and authors I cannot remember. And, of course, with *Under Milk Wood.*

With the onset of adolescence and greater personal mobility, my feeling for books had to compete with more heady passions —I knew of no literary heroines to compete with Gina Lollobrigida or Françoise Arnoul, I knew of no book so resonant of bogus maturity as *La Ronde*, and I suddenly realized that the gratitude of an expectant nation belonged less to John Galsworthy than to Carol Reed, Vittorio de Sica, Jean Renoir and John Huston. I decided to be a film director. The better part of a month was spent writing a film script of John Hersey's

Hiroshima, particularly the first thirty seconds. I must have seen Olivier's Shakespeare films about this time, because I distinctly remember filming *Henry IV*, Parts 1 and 2, while distractedly pacing the windy streets of Edinburgh. I don't know whether my taste was 'good' or not during early adolescence; Christopher Fry was clearly a genius and Eliot, as playwright, a reactionary, wooden bore. Any poetry I may have written owed an amalgamated and baroquely ornate debt to Fry, Pound and Dylan Thomas—I wince to imagine.

Four novels read in leisure during adolescence touched off four shattering implosions: Mailer's *The Naked and the Dead*, Faulkner's *Sanctuary*, Joyce's *Ulysses*, and Dostoyevsky's *Crime and Punishment*.

But I was going to be a film director; an architect; a historian. In the event, I became the historian. This probably means that I have read ten thousand history books and articles since 1952 and don't want to think about any of them, a sentiment not unrelated to the prospect of spending fifty hours of next week in various Oxford libraries. But there is another point. At the time when, at school, I began the serious study of history, the prevailing inclination among history teachers was to treat history as a branch of science, a chronological dimension to a rigorous sociology, rooted in economics, in man's base motives, in demography and scrupulous quibbling about sources. Gibbon or Macaulay or Ranke or Acton might be honoured in the manner of statues, but any contemporary writer who dared to think of historiography as an art, as susceptible to the literary graces, was snarled off the stage. A historian might be respected for what he said, but never, on no account, for the way he said it.

Accordingly, the history books I remember are associated with ideological rather than literary contexts. In so far as I was thinking for myself, I was pursuing Marxism as a total explanation of human behaviour, and exuberantly shooting down all rival explanations—Spengler, Toynbee, Geyl, Butterfield —with deadly materialist bullets. As for Marxism, I did not come to it by way of Marx or Engels, whom I did not seriously read until I was a student or later. I came to it initially along the path of social indignation, via Dickens, Bennett and *Love on the Dole*; later with propulsion from such non-Marxist writers as Shaw, Wells, Tawney and the Hammonds; and finally under the influence of the yellow and magenta Left Book Club exposés I found around the house or in Collet's Bookshop: Haldane, The Red Dean, D. N. Pritt, Cedric Belfrage ... From Collet's I also gleaned a confirmatory collection of sixpenny Soviet pamphlets extolling the advances of Soviet Woman, Soviet Housing, Soviet Education and Soviet Agriculture, as well as a periodical, which I read with considerable enthusiasm, called *Soviet Literature.* It was clear to me that Professor George Thompson's blockheaded description of the class basis of all religious enterprise effectively demolished religion, and that Christopher Hill's description of the class basis of the English Civil War did very much the same. I was not open to argument. In the 'thirties such beliefs put a public school boy in a minority; in the 'fifties they put him in a minority of one. On the whole I found this status congenial and would probably have wavered had anyone close at hand agreed with me. At night I read and re-read Houseman's *A Shropshire Lad,* hiding the book during the day.

Twice I travelled to Oxford to sit the scholarship examination, and both occasions are associated in my mind with a particular book. Arriving at St John's College during the vacation, I was assigned a room whose normal occupant had left behind him a thin scattering of books, paperbacks mostly, one of them caught my eye, I began to read. Of course I should have been in bed early but in the event did not finally crawl between the sheets, bubbling with inexpendable sexual gases, until I had read Alberto Moravia's *The Woman of Rome* from cover to cover. The dawn followed an hour later and it was an ashen surrogate who arrived, uncombed and ruined, in the examination hall. I returned to school garlanded in gammas.

It was my habit to call in at Collet's six times a year, at the beginning and end of each holiday, and the summer following the Moravia fiasco I came upon a gem, published in Moscow, which remains one of my most cherished possessions: *Selected Philosophical Essays*, by N. G. Chernyshevsky. It was Chernyshevsky who first pointed out to me that whereas a delicate, frail physique is considered beautiful among aristocratic women, a ruddy robustness is regarded as more attractive among peasants. Armed with this insight, not to mention its almost limitless implications for aesthetic theory, I subsequently burrowed my ruddy and robust way under the walls of Wadham. And found, on every side, shelves groaning with books and contemporaries who had apparently read and understood every book ever written. I began to read.

MAURICE CRANSTON

In his autobiography, *Les Mots,* Sartre tells us that he grew up, a solitary child, in the company of books, and that because of this he continued long afterwards to assume that the real world was like the world one meets in literature, logical, coherent, purposeful and ordered. This was my own experience. I grew up in a house where books were bits of furniture, never read by anyone except myself; they stood behind glass doors in their depressing Victorian bindings, brown and faintly damp. They included, by some strange chance, a fair number of books by serious writers. I read them all, and from their foxed and yellow pages derived great happiness. The author who impressed me most was Racine.

I never met anyone who shared this preference. People were always ready to discuss Shakespeare or Plato or T. S. Eliot, but at the name of Racine everybody groaned. They all knew, often without ever reading him, that he was a bore; whereas I, who was painfully bored by Scott, Tennyson, Hugo, and other supposedly 'romantic' writers, found Racine both thrilling and compelling. In the textbooks I saw him described as a 'rationalist' whose plays were a stylized representation of the conflict between passion and reason. Yet it seemed obvious to me that *Bérénice* and *Phèdre* and the other plays were all about the conflict between one passion and another. In *Bérénice* it is not duty which triumphs over love (although the protagonists themselves may be making some such claim), but political ambition which triumphs over sexual desire.

I was more sensible, when I was young, of the beauty of the language in Racine than of the moral and psychological insight, but I was already absorbed by the metaphysical theme which ran through much of his work, the antimony of predestination and free will. Racine's philosophical interests were clearly derived from his upbringing under the shadow of Port-Royal and Jansenism; and since the theological teachings of the Low Church, in which I myself was brought up, is akin to Jansenism, and comes down in the same way from St Augustine, I was well prepared to respond to Racine. I also learned from the biographies that Racine's circumstances had been rather like my own, his mother having died when he was very young, and the two institutions with which he was brought into contact at an impressionable age being, as mine were, on the one hand, those of Puritan piety, and on the other, the theatre. In my case, the theatre, having been my father's *métier*, could not be mine, and despite early aspiration to become, like Racine, a dramatist, I was to become a dialectician instead.

My special interest in Racine did not then go together with any general interest in French literature or the thought of the seventeenth century: those two interests developed later. In my first youth, I was more attracted to German writers, especially Hölderlin, Kleist, Rilke and Thomas Mann, all of whose work possessed a metaphysical dimension lacking in English writers of the nineteenth century, except perhaps Coleridge, and conspicuously absent from French writers of that period. I have always loved the novels of Thomas Hardy, and been addicted to Maupassant, but the conception of the universe which both these writers reveal is shamefully jejune and superficial. Hardy's picture of a world controlled by the petty deeds of a cruel God is Sunday-school Christianity inverted, and Maupassant's naive determinism is refuted by his own unforgiving view of human frailty.

My interest in the German writers was shared by a poet I came to know when I was young, Robert Nichols. Since his command of the German language was even worse than mine, he persuaded me to translate for him gobbets of Goethe's *Faust,* a book by which he was obsessed. The result of the exercise for me was a general cooling-off in my zeal for the German authors. Goethe, like Shakespeare, was too much for me, too universal a genius, too overwhelming. I found that my own limitations in this respect were shared by many French critics. I used to turn from Robert Nichols's long, eager, indecipherable letters to read, with feelings of slightly guilty relief, the opinions of those who unashamedly preferred Corneille, Molière and Racine. From that time forth I read hardly any German books at all, except Kant, Hegel and Wittgenstein, who are all, of course, philosophers rather than literary authors.

Robert Nichols was not the first poet I met. In 1934, at the age of fourteen, I had had a conversation with Rudyard Kipling, a weedy-looking man with a strangely radiant soul; and I was much more excited by what he had to say to me than by anything of his I had read in print. My outlook, already influenced by the pamphleteering of people like Maynard Keynes, was anti-imperialist, anti-conservative, anti-war. The ideological content of Kipling proved rebarbative; but the account he gave me of his writing life was riveting. He told me he had left school at sixteen and that before he was twenty he had established himself as a professional writer, with several books and innumerable articles to his credit, and been put up for the Savile Club by Henry James himself.

After this conversation with Rudyard Kipling, I came to be as interested in the literary life as in books, and developed the habit, which is a bad one, of thinking of books as a product of a certain mind and experience, thinking of books as evidence of something beyond themselves about which one needs to learn. A bad habit; but at least it was one which enhanced the appeal of contemporary literature, which, in itself, was not always good in the 1930s. Of course, when one is very young, one likes to read about books that are new from the press. I was disturbed as well as excited by Malraux and Montherlant, and if I had read Sartre's *La Nausée* when it came out in 1938 (when I was eighteen) it would have disturbed me even more. I felt more comfortable with the brighter literature of British liberal humanism: books like Isherwood's *Mr Norris Changes Trains,* Auden's *Letters from Iceland,* Aldous Huxley's *Eyeless in Gaza,* Bertrand Russell's *Freedom and Organization.* Indeed these books helped me so successfully to ram my head into the sand that I hardly noticed that the authors themselves were so far from reassured by their situation that they had discreetly slipped off to America.

Freud's books were still coming out when I was young, and although I thought I was learning a great deal from them, it was many years before I began to understand what Freud really meant. The ruinous defect of Freudian analysis as therapy is that you cannot profit from it unless you have insight, and if you have insight you do not need it; and I think his books do not teach one much, unless one is prepared (I do not mean willing, I mean psychologically prepared) to learn, which means, in a certain sense, that one has to know it already. It took me a very long time to acquire that sort of knowledge. Even so, I read a lot of Freud, and invoked his name in support of a lot of my own foolish remarks about human nature and experience.

And then there was Bloomsbury. I cannot pretend to an unqualified enthusiasm for the novels of Virginia Woolf, but she is clearly the only central member of the Bloomsbury group, apart from Keynes, with claims to greatness. I could never see much merit in the books of Leonard Woolf or Clive Bell, and the work of Lytton Strachey and Roger Fry is surely very slender compared to the size of their reputations. And yet I felt the magnetism of the Bloomsbury *ethos.* On the fringe of Bloomsbury, there were writers I admired more than the

Bloomsbury figures themselves—writers such as Raymond Mortimer, E. M. Forster, Bertrand Russell, Rosamond and John Lehmann, William Plomer, Harold Nicolson and Vita Sackville-West, and then, rather more remote from Bloomsbury, John Middleton Murry and D. H. Lawrence. I did not wholly enjoy Lawrence's novels, but his *Letters* seemed to me to be among the best ever written, almost as good as those of Flaubert, and they still do.

Both Middleton Murry and Bertrand Russell had an undoubted influence on me, and between them changed the central direction of my interests from the literary to the philosophical. The London Civil Defence provided a niche in the war years, but it was not conducive to the awakening of aesthetic sensibilities, and I used to read Descartes and Leibniz in my bunk, and in my hours off duty I attended philosophy lectures at Birkbeck College given by Alec Mace, Ruth Saw and Cyril Joad. Joad was a disgrace as a scholar, but he was good company, and he gave me a glimpse of high socialist intellectual society, where men were like characters in Molière, Joad and Laski being fantastic liars, Leonard Woolf and Kingsley Martin being incredibly mean about money, and so forth.

Bertrand Russell was an altogether nobler character, but no one who had feasted, as I had, on Racine could ever be satisfied with the mind of a late-Victorian Voltaire, and Russell's mind was unredeemed, alas, by Voltaire's pessimism. The disclosures which came at the end of the war, about the Nazi concentration camps, rid me for ever of my old progressive optimism. Koestler's *Darkness at Noon* confirmed my belief that Soviet totalitarianism was almost as bad as Hitler's; George Orwell's arguments in a similar vein appealed to me no less. After the war, Karl Popper, both in his philosophical and his political writings, replaced Russell in my esteem as the most important living philosopher.

Besides, Russell's politics seemed to become more and more outrageous. At one moment he was advocating the use of the atom threat to force Russia into a world government; the next he was whipping up support for Communist aggression in Asia. Everybody was reproaching the Germans for failing to realize what was happening in the Nazi camps, but many of our own progressives were even less excusably unwilling to admit the existence of the Russian camps. Russell was an odd mixture of earnestness and flippancy; the faults he ascribed to Shaw and Lytton Strachey were very much his own. He was a man who lived his life backwards, completing all his great philosophical work before he was forty, and then becoming more and more a social polemicist as he aged into immaturity.

From the charmless ideologies of the twentieth century, I found myself turning more and more to the seventeenth century. Writers like Hobbes and Pascal have no equal in our time; I sometimes wish I had read them when I was young, though I suspect that if I had, I should not have understood them, any more than I understood Freud. My appreciation of Racine was originally more instinctive than intellectual, but he is a writer who has haunted me for forty years. I have no longer any desire to talk about Racine, or read criticisms of him; and yet, if I were allowed to take only one book into solitary confinement with me, I would still choose his *Oeuvres complètes*.

MAUREEN DUFFY

My first literary memory is Rupert, not in the daily strip but read aloud by an aunt from a book, with coloured sugar-paper pages. He is the first too in a whole tribe of animations and cartoon figures who still people my imagination and form elements of my mental furniture: Meddlesome Matty, Lord Snooty and his pals (particularly Snitchy and Snatchy), Desperate Dan, Keyhole Kate, Pinocchio and on through Rat, Mole and company to Kipling's Puck and E. Nesbit's Moldiwarp. From them all, the path leads out into space and the elfland of Romance. They are important because they showed me early on without my realizing that the reality of art needn't be two-dimensional. I found it as easy to suspend my belief in them as in any of the creations of the contemporary social realism of any period. Their mythological brothers and sisters too came easily to me, some of them in the the anthology books I managed to acquire and more in a *Myths and Legends of Many Lands* I still have.

Books were rarely bought except at acknowledged festivals as presents. Those books I owned I had mostly been given second-hand when it became known to workmates and relations that I was 'a reader'. Before I was six I joined the public library and went regularly with my mother, whose passions were Galsworthy, Walpole and Ernest Raymond. My passion at this time and for the next four years was for books about animals, adventure stories and poetry. I dreamt of climbing mountains to see golden eagles hatch or silently watching in night woods for badgers to snuffle out.

I learnt acres of bad poetry, a lot of which is still with me, and began to write my own. At nine I collected what I wanted preserved in a stiff-covered notebook which I still have and from then to fourteen I kept this up so that I have a chronological record of developing craftsmanship and of the poets I had been reading and imitating.

Between ten and eleven I fell in love and this led me deep into Shakespeare's sonnets and to Keats. Daily life was on the whole grim and frightening but it was possible to escape in the imagination and in idealized love. My first encounter with a Shakespeare play, inevitably *A Midsummer Night's Dream,* was deeply disappointing. How could a poet who had written so piercingly the words I muttered as I biked to and from school come down to such triviality? My identification with Keats was almost complete and I still see his influence everywhere in everything I write, both prose and verse. I see too the same see-saw between the real and the ideal but where he splits them, prose (letters) and verse, I run them together perhaps because I've had more time.

At eleven Scott was our class reader and I had at last found a prose writer who could affect me like a poet. Generally I despised prose. I was going to be a poet. So far I had developed imagination more than reason, but the real, the everyday, couldn't be ignored forever. It too had to be grasped and synthesized into a whole consciousness and art. But I disliked the English Classics who might have done this or begun it. They seemed to me unrelated to either my real or ideal. Steadily I added poets: Gerard Manley Hopkins, Eliot, Donne. Desperately I tried other historical writers: Harrison Ainsworth, Bulwer Lytton, Philip Lindsay and Margaret Irwin.

Conrad had replaced Scott as class reader but not for me. Fortunately just in time I found Shaw. He wasn't a novelist but he was at least a prose-writer. He delighted me with his wit, reason and iconoclasm, with the sheer quality and pleasure of the performance. I gave up the attempt to come to terms with The English Novel. Reading the *Prefaces* at thirteen made me feel mature and wicked. Shortly after, I consumed a great deal of Koestler, beginning with *The Yogi and the Commissar*. This too seemed more relevant to observable life.

At fourteen I abandoned formal verse patterns for free or cadenced verse after a long bout of Browning. Pound I had never heard of but our results were technically similar as I discovered when a couple of years later someone accused me of imitating him and I decided to check up.

Somewhere about now I began a Russian diet: the great triumvirate of whom Turgenev was my favourite. It seemed to me that the English couldn't write, hadn't written serious fiction at all. I considered reviving the epic. *Paradise Lost,* which I'd read several times and knew chunks of by heart, was the only great English novel.

Then examination set books began to rain down on me and demand my unwilling attention. More failed English Classics (Hardy and Conrad again) had to be annotated and analyzed. Mercifully there was Shakespeare and the interest of Chaucer's language. For myself I found Helen Waddell. Reality at this point in my life had become intolerable and I was in full Romantic flight, now spiced with sex; *Peter Abelard* and Petronius Arbiter. At seventeen I published my first poems dating from this time two years before.

There was very little more to come. At university, where we were on the whole sadly taught, I discovered *Ulysses*. Perhaps the English, or the Irish, could write fiction after all. In the seminar at which I gave my paper on it I was the only one, including the tutor, who had read the book. My feeling of wicked sophistication revived but it was the excitement of the Joycean techniques that really took hold of me. There was no need it seemed to write a novel in one key or style. And everything could go in: myth, metaphysics, poetry, the insides and outsides of people's heads and guts, sex, religion. It was an enormous liberation. Not that I wanted to write novels. I was half way through a Neo-Jacobean play about a railway strike that would bring back concrete imagery to the theatre.

J. G. FARRELL

I should like, at this great distance of years, to pay tribute to the enlightened person whose job it was to choose French text-books for use in schools round about 1948. For in that year, or perhaps it was a year or two after, he chose, among others, Pierre Loti's *Pêcheur d'Islande*. It was a dull green text-book, no more exciting in appearance than the French grammar of an earlier stage which catalogued the bourgeois doings of a pair of odious French kids called Marcel and Denise at fashionable places like Deauville. It was impossible at first sight to recognize in this green book the trap door through which, without in the least intending to, I would crawl into another culture. To the colleagues of the enlightened man or woman who chose it, this novel must have seemed an odd selection, for Loti's reputation, still considerable in the 'twenties, had gone into a sharp decline in the years before the last war and by 1948 it must have touched bottom. Today one seldom comes across anyone who has read Loti, even in France. The blend of poetry and exoticism which so appealed to our grandparents has now altogether lost its hold over us, its power diminished equally by the ease of travel and the spread of Western civilization to the remote parts visited by Loti.

'At his best,' says Edmund Gosse in the *Encyclopaedia Britannica* of 1911, 'Pierre Loti was unquestionably the finest descriptive writer of the day. In the delicate exactitude with which he reproduced the impression given to his own alert nerves by unfamiliar forms, colours, sounds and perfumes, he was without a rival. But he was not satisfied with this exterior charm; he desired to blend with it a moral sensibility of the extremest refinement, at once sensual and ethereal. Many ot his best books are long sobs of remorseful memory, so personal, so intimate, that an English reader is amazed to find such depth of feeling compatible with the power of minutely and publicly recording what is felt.'

Shortly after we had begun to read *Pêcheur d'Islande* in the classroom I realized with surprise that I was becoming intensely interested in this story of Breton fishermen and their difficulties. Presently it became clear to me that our corporate progress as a class was too slow and I took to poring over the book in my spare time (a hobby which my class-mates interpreted as a sign of imminent mental collapse), looking up unfamiliar words, of which there were a great number, in a dictionary. But soon even this became too slow, and I simply read on and on, ignoring or guessing the words I did not know. Very often the meanings I attributed to words were entirely my own, but that hardly seemed to matter. So powerful an impression did this book make on me that even today there are certain phenomena for which an expression of Loti's will alone suffice. A certain wintry light over the sea, for example, still conjures up Loti's '*lumière blafarde*'. I had no idea then, nor have I now, of the precise meaning of *blafard*. In my own mind it bears such perfect witness as it is, that to find its accepted meaning might prove an inconvenience.

When I had finished *Pêcheur d'Islande* I embarked on other books by Loti; at one time you frequently came across them n second-hand bookshops in Dublin in the company of other once-popular works whose readership had undergone a similar shrinkage, Stevenson's *Virginibus Puerisque,* Tennyson's *Col-*

lected Works, or Samuel Smiles's *Self-Help.* Although somewhat less enthralling as stories than *Pêcheur d'Islande* the novels that I read subsequently by Loti had to an even greater degree the sensuality which Gosse noticed in his work and which was apparent even to the veiled comprehension of the child reading him for the first time. *Madame Chrysanthème,* which describes a visit Loti paid to Japan, and *Aziyadé,* a semi-autobiographical flirtation in Constantinople with a lady from a harem, were manifestly unlike anything I had ever read in English and prepared me for an adolescent devotion to Colette.

There was another novel which I first read even younger (I would guess about the age of eight or nine). This was Richard Hughes's *In Hazard.* It describes a ship going through a great storm and bears a superficial resemblance to Conrad's *Typhoon.* I can still remember the feverish excitement with which I read it as a child. Some twenty years later I came across an old copy of it in the British Council Library in Paris and read it again with no less excitement as an adult. How many novels are there which are capable of inducing in both a child and an adult that special state of narcosis which accompanies a complete surrender to the author's design? The virtues of Richard Hughes's writing, the relaxed tone, the hallucinating clarity of image, and the concreteness that gives substance to his vision, are qualities which he shares with Conrad at his best. Let me give an example, taken from Conrad's *Heart of Darkness,* of the qualities I mean. How could this description, a reminiscence of the narrator making his way down the coast of Africa by sea, be bettered as an image of uphill colonialism?

> Once, I remember, we came upon a man-of-war anchored off the coast. There wasn't even a shed there, and she was shelling the bush. It appears the French had one of their wars going on thereabouts. Her ensign dropped limp like a rag; the muzzles of the long six-inch guns stuck out all over the low hull; the greasy, slimy swell swung her up lazily and let her down, swaying her

thin masts. In the empty immensity of earth, sky, and water, there she was, incomprehensible, firing into a continent. Pop, would go one of the six-inch guns; a small flame would dart and vanish, a little white smoke would disappear, a tiny projectile would give a feeble screech—and nothing happened. Nothing could happen. There was a touch of insanity in the proceeding ...

There are, it is agreed, a hundred thousand ways of writing a novel and an equal variety of intentions that may be given substance in a novel. A reader may pick and choose among this variety as great a number as he wants, but ordinarily a writer must choose only one way to write. This being so, I believe (subject to all possible later changes of mind) that the qualities of Conrad and Hughes are those which accord most closely to my own conception of what goes to make a good novel.

It now seems to me, in retrospect, that it rained ceaselessly every day throughout my Irish adolescence. Reason tells me that this is impossible. My unlikely recollection is, nevertheless, that for five or six years I sat by a streaming window pane reading Colette, in a state which combined great lethargy and an acute sensitivity to the sensual world. *Chéri* bewildered me. What exactly was going on? And what were Claudine and her friends actually *doing* to each other? My insufficient knowledge of French lay over her intimate life like a heavy veil, permitting fruitful speculation. The mysterious sexuality of Colette's prose seemed to be, as novelists used to say, 'in the very air I breathed'. And then one day, one year, it stopped raining at last, the clouds rolled away, and I stepped out into the watery sunlight of the real world, anxious to stop day-dreaming and get on with it, whatever 'it' might turn out to be.

JOHN FOWLES

Some years ago I decided to get myself a book-plate. It wasn't quite pure vanity, for part of the pleasure of book-collecting lies in the awareness of past ownerships, and I like to think of some browser of the twenty-second century (if books and browsers still then exist) coming on my plate in a volume he fancies. There was the question of design: a general emblem for the sort of book I enjoy possessing. Various elegant motifs were proposed by the woodcut artist. But in the end only one, not at all elegant, seemed appropriate; I now have a plate that shows my name surrounded by magpies.

Every treatise on bibliomania repeats the same excellent advice—stick to one age, one field, one press, one author ... specialize or waste your money. All mine has gone down the drain, since I have never bought for editions or bindings or printers, and even less for literary standing. All I have are waifs and strays, a broken-backed detritus from the last four centuries, and most of which the rest of the world has quite rightly consigned to oblivion. My lack of decent reading has become increasingly embarrassing. I am faced with it every time I meet students, and the vast uncharted spaces in my knowledge of the contemporary—and the classical—novel are revealed. When humiliated beyond endurance, I sometimes pretend that apart from one or two old favourites, like Defoe, Austen and Peacock, I much prefer bad novels to good ones. In one sense that is true. A bad novel tells you more about the age it was written in than a good one—a proposition so blasphemous to the average classic-stuffed Strasbourg goose, alias academic, that it must be correct.

Unkind; but at least it leads me to a shadow of a first connecting principle in my own reading. Above all I like a book to give me the sharp feel of the age it was written in, which is one reason I prefer early editions, however imperfect, to the best-annotated modern ones. Textual accuracy and apparatus attract me far less than the idea that this is how the book 'felt' when the writer was still alive; and this in turn is because I regard the kind of books I collect as space- or time-machines: examples of science fiction in reverse, glimpses of an unknown past. Only a few weeks ago I picked up for less than a pound a coverless but otherwise complete descending of hair by the key witness at a French murder trial of 1817. During the trial the lady had broken down and changed testimony, and got an exceedingly bad name for herself; and the *Mémoire* is an attempt on Clarisse Manson's part to explain her behaviour to the world before the appeal hearing. To do that she recounts in every detail where she was and what she did on the days surrounding the murder; and suddenly the miracle takes place, one is back in the March of 1817, in the remote town of Rodez in the Aveyron, and inside the mind of a neurotically intelligent and self-dramatizing young Frenchwoman. For me such reading experiences are very like landing on another, *and* inhabited, planet.

Or I think of another recent buy: *An Enquiry into, and Detection of the Barbarous Murther of the late Earl of Essex*. Officially the Earl committed suicide about 9 a.m. on the morning of July 13th, 1683; but this long pamphlet of 1689 sets out to show he was murdered by the establishment papists. It was written by 'Plotter' Ferguson, a vitriolic polemicist of the Puritan New Left in the late seventeenth century. He re-creates that July morning and then analyzes its events with all the sharp eye for conflicting detail and the contemptuous scepticism of a Sherlock Holmes. Once again the reading leaps the imagination back over three centuries—both into the strange and grisly mystery of Essex's death and the oddly proleptic political anger that drove Ferguson and his kind.

Old trials, travel books and historical memoirs provide this experience far more vividly than any other category. Novels, alas, are very rarely half as convincing and exciting. Yet I believe my predilection for the kind of true history described above does help me in writing my own fiction. The great bulk of such reading willy-nilly steeps the mind in narrative technique—and not the artificial inventions of the novelist, but the real thing. Good memoirists often show an economy of characterization, a swiftness of narrative pace, an ear for the kernel of dialogue, that puts the mere fictioneer to shame. I know I have learnt a lot from them.

I also hate books that can be put down; and if they have no narrative to sustain them then they had better, so far as I am concerned, be bloody good in other directions. Narrative is my second connective principle in choice of reading. I have an unlimited greed for it, which seriously distorts my literary judgment. An abysmally low boredom threshold has prevented me from ever finishing countless serious and worthy novels by serious and worthy authors. I can admire people like Richardson and George Eliot, but I could never read them for pleasure. All this makes it difficult for me to answer questions about influence.

I would admit it, in a direct and singular sense, of only one of my own books—the first in writing, though not in the publishing. *The Magus* is a kind of homage to *Le Grand Meaulnes*—but even that flawed masterpiece (whose faults I can see, whose deep emotional hold on me I cannot understand) had usurped another, the first book I ever loved passionately and almost totally lived—and which I think I should have to name, on quasi-archetypal grounds, if one is limited to a unique master-influence. That is Richard Jefferies' *Bevis*. I still consider it the best boys' story in the language; and the fact that not one child in a million today has read it I regard as their loss, not proof of my faulty judgment.

I have in any case no memory at all for novels, for their ideas, plots and characters. I could not even reconstitute my own with any accuracy if I were obliged to. I suppose I read as I write. I live the direct and present experience very intensely; but when it is over, it sinks very rapidly out of sight. So all I can honestly offer is a couple of dozen shelves of magpie nonsense, nine-tenths forgotten by everyone else and even by myself in every but some very remote and rare-snagging sense. Let me pick down a few at random ...

Mémoires de Trenck, 1789, a great prison escape story; *Roswall and Lillian*, the 1822 reprint, Swinburne's copy; *Menagiana*, pirated 1693, full of good anecdotes; *Tell It All*, 1878, an anti-Mormon classic; the *Sporting Magazine* for 1816, splendid on the 'fancy'; *The Diaboliad*, 1777, a furious squib by William Combe; *The Wild Party*, privately printed in 1929, a very odd piece of Jazz Age doggerel I am not alone in admiring; a reprint of the Bedford Eyre Roll for 1227, a real time-machine; *On the Height of the Aurora Borealis*, 1828, John Dalton and signed by him; *Account of a visit to Rome*, 1899, manuscript and hilariously priggish; *Mémoires de Martin du Bellay*, 1573, Joachim's uncle, with an eye-witness account by the old boy of the Field of the Cloth of Gold; *Pidgin English Sing-Song*, 1876 ('Littee Jack Horner/Makee sit inside corner/Chow-chow he Clismas pie ... '); *Candide*, 1761, Geneva, containing the first edition of the spurious second part; *Lost Countess Falka*, 1897, a yellow-back by Richard Henry Savage and currently my nomination for the worst novel in the English language; the *Mercure Galant* for September, 1685, with a fascinating account of how the Bolognese dwarfed their spaniels (they immersed the puppies daily in *eau-de-vie*, then bashed their noses in); *Souvenir Programme of the Cornish Gorsedd of the Bards*, 1938; *An Essay on the Art of Ingeniously Tormenting*, 1804 ...

That seems a fitting title on which to stop, and I will spare you all the other forgotten plays, travels, memoirs, murders and what-not I have accumulated over the years. I am afraid this cannot seem serious; and yet it is more so than you may think. A novelist must, I believe, extend *humani nihil alienum* to books as well. A quite literal pair of magpies breeds in my garden every year. Wicked creatures though they are, I let them be. One must not harm one's own.

BAMBER GASCOIGNE

In all fairness I must open with *The Wooden Horse* by Eric Williams. A surprising start but it happened to be the only book I read for pleasure between the ages of thirteen and sixteen, my one taste in that crucial period of the miraculous late-for-meals long-on-the-lavatory seized-by-a-book feeling which a reader always searches for and a writer must hope to give. I was in an obstinately anti-intellectual frame of mind and enraged my long-suffering housemaster by keeping in my desk the leg of a hare and the wing of a pheasant with which, on a tiny vice, I constructed flies to catch trout. I picked up *The Wooden Horse* one day at home, and for twenty-four ecstatic hours sport was forgotten. It didn't have the immediate effect of sending me back to literature, but it remained as a powerful memory of what books can do. My loyal and infinitely subtle wife tells me that if I want to get better reviews for a novel I must make my next one rather more boring. She may well be right about catching critics. But Eric Williams knew which flies to cast for the readers.

Apart from this hallowed memory I can only think of compiling my list, an inevitably random affair, by choosing favourites within particular categories.

Store-houses of magnificent phrases. There is no one to beat the seventeenth-century prose writers and particularly, for me, Sir Thomas Browne and Robert Burton. Nor are their delights, as is often charged against Browne, merely those of quaintness. Browne: 'Generations pass while some trees stand, and old families last not three oaks'; or 'The long habit of living in-disposeth us for dying.' Burton: 'Their dugs like double jugs, or else, in that other extreme, no dugs at all.'

Books which linger in the mind by virtue of their charm. A particular favourite is *Lark Rise to Candleford,* Flora Thompson's account of life in the Oxfordshire village which she knew as a child in the 1880s. Among diarists Parson Woodforde has this same effect on me—surprisingly, perhaps, since in many ways he was an unsympathetic and bigoted cleric (with a parish in Norfolk in the late eighteenth century), but his fascination with every small detail of the life going on about him excuses all. Famous names are at least an important prop in Pepys, and almost the object of the exercise in Evelyn; James Woodforde carries one along with only his niece Nancy, his servant Ben, a succession of plain and generally unsatisfactory servant girls, and all the many neighbours who drop in to join him for the gigantic meals in which he takes such pleasure. In this same category I would add the recent series of photographic books which began with Gordon Winter's *A Country Camera* 1844–1914 and which has continued with the Batsford collections of Victorian and Edwardian photographs of individual counties. Nothing is so evocative as old photographs. That very instant, that particular setting, those people, the bodies beneath those clothes, the visible hints of wishes, impulses, relationships, even the guessable moment immediately before and the moment immediately after, all these undeniably existed in a way that can never be so true of a verbal description or a painting.

Fables. I have a weakness for fables, particularly at that point where they begin to overlap with the novel. *Lord of the Flies* is a perfect example, and coming nearer to the form of the traditional fable *Animal Farm* has to be a favourite. For many years I worshipped *Candide*, but on re-reading it recently I was disappointed to find it arbitrary and feeble. Voltaire's intentions too visibly control his choice of events. In a good fable it is the other way round—the story seems effortlessly to make the point. Nevertheless, *Candide* retains its place by virtue of another powerful schoolboy memory. It provided my first realization that books can be distinctly saucy and yet be admired as literature. One of the ladies smuggles some diamonds by hiding them *'où nous autres femmes n'attendent que des canules'*. *Canules, canules* ... idly I turned the pages of the dictionary during prep and was astounded to find '*Med:* Nozzle (of syringe)'. Hardly very stimulating now, but in those days enough to set the schoolboy mind racing.

Biographies. There is a new style of long, serious, 'definitive' biography which borrows the freedom of the nineteenth-century novel in its construction, allowing full play to the tiniest details of the subject's everyday life and arranging the material in a pattern of climax and suspense more familiar in fiction. The old style of definitive biography (Mrs Gaskell on Charlotte Brontë is a classic of this type, and there have been plenty since) is content to quote long extracts from documents when they fall due in the chronological sequence; the new style quotes them, usually in shorter extracts, where they will best contribute to the story. A magnificent example was Michael Holroyd's *Lytton Strachey*, and Elizabeth Longford used the form brilliantly (on a subject too vast for anyone to aim at the definitive) in her *Victoria R.I.* But perhaps my favourite—aptly enough, since the subject herself perfected the fictional techniques which I believe these biographers inherit—is Gordon Haight's *George Eliot*.

Oddities. There are certain books which one loves immoderately because hardly anyone else seems to have heard of them. My choice here would be Stanley Crawford's *Gascoyne*, and I deny being influenced by the name. It is a first novel published in 1966 and tells of an irrepressible character, Gascoyne, who runs a vast and tumbledown commercial empire from an even more tumbledown jalopy equipped with a radio telephone. Some extracts from the first four pages: 'It all starts when I give thc accelerator pedal a couple of pumps and turn the ignition key and the starter growls and finally the engine turns over and comes to life with noises that aren't as regular as they used to be. The old Nash which is the last big one they made back in '55 is getting a little tired but I'm faithful to the end and won't let the buggy out of my hands until it gets to the point where she just won't go any more. Just then the phone rings. ... I slip the thing into drive and squeeze my way into Bastinado Street traffic mess and run it up to thirty-five, which is what everybody is trying to do in spite of the fact they haven't got around to synchronizing the signals yet. But if you try to go slow they start rubbing the chrome off your rear bumper. Then the phone rings again. ... I hit the two lights at about fifty and catch the green arrow left on to Mirindaranda Road, which runs east out into the sticks ... The traffic looks reasonable for the hour and then the thing is six lanes wide so it pretty well handles the shopping traffic, being as it is one of those continuous commercial boulevards with drive-in everything for ten miles, open twenty-four hours a day. I give Chester a ring.' Already it reads like a fond valediction to the world of the 'sixties, those days when oil sheikhs were still figures of fun.

Is there a black list as well, of negative influences so strong as to prove formative? I would cite only philosophy, a subject in which I find that all statements which are not obvious are incomprehensible and any statement which ceases to be incomprehensible becomes obvious. My Penguin of Plato still bears the scar of where I flung it against a Cambridge wall, finally exasperated beyond endurance by one of the yes-men kept on a retainer to spar with Socrates.

I will end with a couple of poets—Robert Henryson and William Dunbar, the so-called Scottish Chaucerians of the late fifteenth century. Many books had made me want to write books, but it was Dunbar's famous poem *Lament for the Makers* which first made attractive the idea—particularly relevant to this volume—of being a writer among other writers. Dunbar opens his poem by saying that he has fallen ill, and looking around him he sees that Death spares none, not princes or prelates, not captains, clerks, astrologers, doctors—not even writers. The remaining verses are his lament for the poets, coming with every line perilously closer to himself.

He has done petuously devour
The noble Chaucer, of makaris flour,
The Monk of Bury, and Gower, all three:—
Timor Mortis conturbat me.

Chaucer had died about a century before. Since then, Dunbar continues, the fell scorpion Death has carried off the good Sir Hew of Eglinton, Sir Mungo Lockhart of the Lee, Blind Harry, Sandy Traill and many others:

He has reft Merseir his endite,
That did in luve so lively write,
So short, so quick, of sentence hie:—
Timor Mortis conturbat me.

He has tane Rowll of Aberdene,
And gentill Rowll of Corstorphine;
Two better fallowis did no man see:—
Timor Mortis conturbat me.

In Dunfermline he has done roun
With Maister Robert Henrysoun;
Sir John the Ross enbrast has he:—
Timor Mortis conturbat me.

Good Maister Walter Kennedy
In point of Death lies verily;
Great ruth it were that so suld be:—
Timor Mortis conturbat me.

Sen he has all my brether tane,
He will naught let me live alane;
Of force I man his next prey be:—
Timor Mortis conturbat me.

Maister Robert Henrysoun, mourned by Dunbar, can follow on well from that, for he provided one of the least solemn death-bed scenes ever recorded. If words are our business, as writers, why not last words too? We cannot leave them all to the statesmen and generals, monarchs and courtesans. Sir Francis Kynaston recorded in 1635 this traditional version of Henryson's death:

> This Mr Robert Henryson he was questionles a learned and witty man, and it is pitty we have no more of his works, because being very old he dyed of a diarrhoea or fluxe, of whom there goes this merry, though somewhat unsavoury tale, that all phisitians having given him over and he lying drawing his last breath there came an old woman unto him, who was held a witch, and asked him whether he could be cured, to whome he sayed very willingly, then quod she there is a whikey tree in the lower end of your orchard, and if you will goe and walk but thrice about it, and thrice repeate theis wordes whikey tree whikey tree take away this fluxe from me you shall be presently cured, he told her that beside he was extreme faint and weake it was extreme frost and snow and that it was impossible for him to go: she told him that unles he did so it was impossible he should recover. Mr Henrysoun then lifting up himselfe, and pointing to an oken table that was in the roome, asked her and seied gude dame I pray ye tell me, if it would not do as well if I repeated thrice theis words oken burd oken burd garre me shit a hard turde. The woman seeing herself derided and scorned ran out of the house in a great passion and Mr Henrysoun within a halfe a quarter of an houre departed this life.

BRIAN GLANVILLE

The Books I Read

I have always suspected that authors lie about the books they read, their purported influences, much as men lie about their sex lives; they are at once ashamed and vain, reluctant to be judged, hiding behind a safe parapet of Joyce and Proust and Kafka. I shall try, then, to be honest.

When I was eight, I read Robert Louis Stevenson—*Treasure Island, Kidnapped, Catriona*—the *Wizard,* the *Skipper,* the *Rover,* the *Hotspur, Adventure* and the *Champion.* The reading of 'good' books can, often does, grow out of the compost of the bad.

When I was nine, I read nonsense like Bulldog Drummond and the Saint. I had long been reading the William books, and continued long to do so. I was also reading Dennis Wheatley.

At ten, one of his—I was going to say absurd—occult novels called *Strange Conflict* seemed to me the most exciting book I'd ever read; but then when I was nine a Saint book called *The Last Hero* had seemed the most moving and tragic book I'd ever read. Perhaps *Strange Conflict,* with its Haitian satanist, its astral adventures, would indeed seem absurd if I read it now; what matters is that it was exciting and stimulating when I read it then. *Habent sua fata libelli,* in a writer's life as well as their own. Do I not remember Graham Greene confessing that one of the most germinal books of his adolescence was Marjorie Bowen's *Viper of Milan*?

From Stevenson's Scottish romances I went on, at the age of nine or ten, to the *New Arabian Nights,* Dr Jekyll and the rest, yet the only book, of all these, which has stayed with me is *Treasure Island*; so much so that in some strange way, I have never been able to see it straight, to decide, even when re-reading it, just where it belongs, whether it is good or, in Orwell's phrase, good-bad, literature, whether it is a magnificent tale for children or a flawed book for adults.

Behind such confusion quite clearly lies a wish, or a resistance, and the resistance is no doubt to destroying by analysis something cherished. Whatever the prevailing views on character in the novel, there can be no doubt that Long John Silver has ebulliently survived, a marvellous grotesque, a romantic villain. For the boy reader, identification with Jim Hawkins is easy and strong, but it is Long John Silver who remains, even to the extent of perpetual impersonations on the television screen; a kind of literary archetype.

It was at prep school that one began reading the enormous *œuvre* of P. G. Wodehouse, continuing to read it through public school and a little beyond. Not much further beyond. Again, I hesitate to dismiss books which once gave me great pleasure, yet I have found the serious praise of Wodehouse by serious English writers a silly affectation, or perhaps a lacuna. He is a splendid entertainer, Jeeves and Psmith and Ukridge delightful conceits, but none has the stature of a great comic figure, of a Micawber or a Falstaff, just as the context in which they are to be found lies outside the domain of literature. Nor does it, to its creator's credit, pretend to lie anywhere else. How often did I go back to *Psmith Journalist* in my early teens, how happily share the adventures of Ukridge, Bertie Wooster and Mike, that stolid cricketer, but I cannot go back to them now: again, for what it matters.

The William stories I read for more than ten years, and I can still remember the saga of George Porgie in his white sailor suit, bluffed by the Outlaws into being smothered with mud, and mouthing strange oaths before a horrified audience of once admiring mothers. William had a remarkably long run, though the spark seemed to go out of Richmal Crompton's books at the beginning of the last war. They are still read; though not by my own children, who leave the William books I bought them politely alone, like a fastidious cat with a saucer of sour milk. When I glance at the books now, they seem pompous.

After these, there was Conan Doyle; not merely Sherlock Holmes, though of course one worshipped and cherished him, but also the historical romances which Doyle himself placed high above Holmes; and even, about the age of fourteen, *The Land of Mist*, his propagandist melodrama of the occult. How one throbbed in sympathy!

Shakespeare one reveres yet takes somehow for granted, his plays the warp and woof of the reading of any English child brought up in prep and public schools, a perpetual, immanent presence since the age of about twelve, the poetry growing and expanding in the mind, to dwarf almost everything around it.

Dickens I met first, only in the form of *A Christmas Carol,* beautifully and ritually read each year, on dark December evenings, by my prep-school headmaster. Not till I was sixteen did I turn to the other novels and devour them; with the exception of *A Tale of Two Cities,* which we read in class, and which disappointed me. *Great Expectations* I first read, with huge enjoyment, only when I was nineteen.

At thirteen, what may now appear another protracted aberration: Gerald Kersh. On the inside flap of almost all his book jackets was a quotation from John Brophy: 'A writer of power and fury.' It is hard now to appreciate that he had such a vogue during the last war, yet I am forever meeting people of about my own age who confess to having shared the same guilty passion; to having rows of his novels tucked away on lower shelves. I was 'hooked', I suppose, for about five years. There was, I now see, no ghost of a shaping artistic conscience at work, no attempt to mould and discipline what was unquestionably a robust and racy natural talent, but much of it read vividly, then: the tales of Bill Nelson and the Guardsmen, the gamey reminiscences of Bohemian life in Soho, some of the short stories, meretricious though they were. Certainly he 'knew the world'; certainly he had vigour and drive, though what one may have learned from him was probably dangerous.

At eighteen I discovered Evelyn Waugh, reading and endlessly re-reading the early satires; *Decline and Fall* I took up again each January. *Scoop* and *Black Mischief* seemed funny beyond belief. The elaborate snobberies of *Brideshead Revisited* and *A Handful of Dust* were less grateful, but how one responded to the misfortunes of Paul Pennyfeather, the misadventures of William Boot; to such scattered jewels as that of the ancient Nanny who had a habit of 'bringing off showy doubles in the flat season'.

I was eighteen, too, when an aunt brought me a Penguin copy of *The Great Gatsby,* then a forgotten novel, saying, almost apologetically, that though the book was unpretentious, the characters somehow stayed in the mind. I was captivated by its lambent romance, its fine economy, racing on from there to *The Crack-Up*, then barking my toes on what I still consider to be the mediocrity of the rest of Fitzgerald's work. If I may include a long short story in my list, it was at this age, too, that I was swept away by Thomas Mann's *Mario and the Magician.*

Nineteen was the age at which I encountered George Orwell, who influenced my thinking—rather than my writing—much as he influenced most of my English literary generation. Politically, I was weaned away from the selfish snobberies left by a public school conditioning by the description of working down the mine in *The Road to Wigan Pier*. *Animal Farm* still seems perfect to me in its way, bringing off the extraordinary trick of being, ultimately, a satire which involves the heart as well as the head, and I am perpetually returning to those incomparable essays.

At about the same time, I developed a taste for early Isherwood. He, too, was introduced to me, when a temporarily forgotten writer, in the form of a Penguin—lent to me by an Ulster journalist who pronounced it agreeably urbane. It was *Mr Norris Changes Trains,* another book I frequently re-read, along with *Lions and Shadows* and *Goodbye to Berlin,* though I have never brought myself to read the later novels, happy to remain with Sally Bowles, Herr Issyvoo and the awful Nowaks.

The cataclysmic discovery of Freud did not take place till I was twenty-three and living in Rome. I began, conventionally, with the *Introductory Lectures* and sat reading them, transfixed, morning after morning, in my ugly little furnished flat in Prati, among the bulbous, Victorian furniture, a parody of the world from which he had wanted to liberate his readers and patients. If I say it was a revelation, it was a partial one, to the extent that I realized just how much of one's thinking and assumptions had already been shaped by Freud. The personality which shone through his pages was exquisitely sympathetic; of a sublime honesty, an astonishing percipience, an immense intellectual force. I read, quite simply, every book he had written, from the *Interpretation of Dreams* through the complete *Collected Papers,* and on through such crystalline speculations as *Leonardo* and *Moses and Monotheism.*

Since then, and those exciting days, the book which has most stimulated and compelled me is Norman O. Brown's meta-Freudian *Life Against Death.* Professor Brown purports to be more of an optimist than Freud in his *Civilization and Its Discontents,* but in fact he is immensely more pessimistic, despite his cries for a 'Dionysiac Ego', locating, in his brilliant analysis, the troubles of the psyche in psycho-physiological processes which are simply beyond reach: if you wish, in Freud's 'constitutional factor'.

The list is quite incomplete. It should really contain the lamented *John o'London's Weekly* which I began to read when I was ten, and which once turned down a poem of mine at that age, telling me gently that if I persevered and read the works of the great masters, 'one day you may find many publishers'. Indeed I did, but it was not for poetry.

I should perhaps have mentioned an addiction to Poe when I was twelve, the years with Faulkner, a decade later, and my concurrent affection for Joyce Cary, who deserves to be better remembered. I am sure I learned from Graham Greene, though the parts seem far greater than the whole. I was riveted, in my early twenties, by the poignant reminiscences of Arthur Koestler, enthralled by *Darkness at Noon.*

But I am grateful, in different ways and for different benefactions, to them all.

PATRICIA HIGHSMITH

An American Book-Bag

My family says that I read nursery rhymes fluently aged two, but probably I knew them by heart. The earliest reading I can recall is the newspaper account of Floyd Collins's mishap in a Kentucky cave, or maybe it was in Tennessee. This was in 1925 when I was four. Floyd Collins, a hillbilly boy now celebrated in a ballad, had discovered a natural cavern near where he lived, and with an eye to exploiting it commercially, had ventured to explore it alone. In a narrow passage, a stone smaller than a loaf of bread (which I later held in my hands, aged ten, when my family drove through that area) fell across his ankle, pinning him hopelessly. Rescue teams dug, food was passed down to him, but neither he nor anyone else could reach his ankle. I remember racing barefoot in my dropseat overalls down the hall to pick up the *Fort Worth Star-Telegram* from the front porch, and racing back to the kitchen to read aloud to my Scots grandmother, who at 7 a.m. would be standing at the stove, stirring a pot of oatmeal. This was my first adventure story, strung out with all the suspense of instalments. The thrill is still with me, and a memory of anxiety and sympathy for the young man trapped.

Around age five, I remember *Merton of the Movies,* a popular novel about Hollywood, full of real-life photographs. On the nose of one of the blonde, cupid's-bow-lipped beauties, a little girl chum and I succeeded in smashing a large housefly by slamming the book shut. Gales of mirth! I eschewed the formidable Shakespeare on my grandmother's shelves, and pored over a thick, blue-bound volume called *The Great War,* or perhaps *The World War.* There'd been only one then. It had three or four clumps of photographs which I found riveting: a cavalry charge that had ended in a mass of horses and men in a muddy ditch; wounded soldiers borne on stretchers; rows of French Blue Berets marching smartly; portraits of Woodrow Wilson, Pershing and Foch. And names like Ypres and Verdun. I also read the prose, and the jingoistic poems, written to recruit soldiers, I still recall.

By six I was in New York and entered school. I don't remember any interesting school reading matter, except *Sesame and Lilies* (Ruskin) when I was ten, which I actually enjoyed. Even when I was twelve, my class was ploughing through *The Last of the Mohicans*, spending two weeks on one chapter. There were many Italians in New York then, and refugees whose language was German or Yiddish, so reading in English was a slow procedure. But at home, I had my mother's and stepfather's books to browse in. They both worked, I had the house to myself after 3.30 p.m., and as far as I know no books were ever hidden from me, nor was any effort made by any adult at any time to make me read this or that. Carl Menninger I remember best. I think the title was *The Human Mind.* This book had twelve-line paragraphs in dark print, summarizing a man's or woman's life story plus their deranged behaviour, and I think stated whether they were cured or not. At any rate, the book made a great impression on me, though I did not realize it at the time. I did not think of deranged people as dangerous or frightening. I was simply amazed by the scope and variations of the personality.

From eight to nine, I was back in Texas, staying at my

grandmother's house, and going to a local school called Sixth Ward. One hour a week came 'library hour', in which we learned how to check out books and to return them. We must have been allowed to choose or browse, because I remember this was my American Indian period, I took Indian books home, and in the 'library hour' I went at once to a certain shelf and resumed the book or books I had been reading the week before. It was the independence of the Indians that appealed to me, the delightful knowledge that they found their own food by hunting, slept in tepees, bathed when and if they pleased, wore leather clothes, rode horses bareback, and made their own weapons, bows and arrows which killed with hardly a sound. Who could be on the white man's side? The Indians had a right to their land. At this time also *The Boy Allies* fell into my hands—somehow, because certainly no school would have recommended this series. *The Boy Allies Behind the Lines, Under Foreign Skies,* and so forth. This unlikely pair of rather goody-goody American boys were fast friends and had a tree house or club house behind the house of one of their parents, where they met to discuss their next enterprise. A letter would have come, a cry of distress from someone in Europe. The First World War was on, but America had not yet entered, or if America had entered, the boys were too young to join up but wanted to fight anyway. Off they went to France (by boat it must have been, which logically should have taken some of the steam out of them), and adventures followed of which I recall absolutely nothing, but they were fun to read, and as for identification, it was total.

Back in New York aged nine and ten, it was Jack London, *Little Women*, R. L. Stevenson, and books such as *Prester John*. The illustrations of Howard Pyle and N. C. Wyeth made that world complete. A pirate on a tilting deck, the good captain with a knife at his throat at the hands of a villain with bared teeth—how wonderful it was to be alive and read such things, which came in endless supply from the public library. Sherlock Holmes and the magic gaslit world of an England I had never seen, England where people talked in such a complicated way and yet so clearly. I succumbed again to series, one about a cadet at West Point which I devoured, another about an English boy named Jeremy (*Jeremy at Crale,* etc.) which inspired me to refuse French before I'd started Latin in my school. I was eleven. I am still amazed that I stood up for myself, saying that Latin logically came before French and besides, that was the way they did things in England. I was told firmly that I could have no Latin before I was fourteen. So I sat out French classes in the school library, reading such things as Hazlitt's essays and Boswell's *Life of Samuel Johnson.* By thirteen I was allowed Latin. I remember my first grammar—clean and new, oddly enough for school issue. Opposite the title page was a golden key in a casket or box, a colour photograph, with the legend below: 'Latin is the golden key to language.' I felt my education had begun, if a bit late.

I should mention that when I was eleven, an unusual privilege was bestowed on me: I was allowed to take books from the adult section of the local Andrew Carnegie Public Library. This was in Astoria, Long Island, still a part of Greater New York. Maybe this honour was conferred because I always came to the library alone, and may have had a quiet manner. Anyway, I remember being told not to tell my friends that I was allowed to take adult books out. I plunged at once into the psychology section, took books out, and often sat reading books which were not allowed to be borrowed. I must have had a two-month period of this before it tapered off. I never took a course in psychology in university, however. I believe it is an art, not a science, therefore I prefer the browsing approach.

At fifteen, I met a couple of intellectual girls at my high school. These two plumped for Hemingway, Katherine Mansfield, Proust and T. S. Eliot. I appreciate Hemingway now as a literary milestone, but I never loved his work. Thomas Wolfe I liked better. Then there were dips into Rosamund Lehmann and Elizabeth Bowen, whose writings are impossible for a fifteen-year-old, who has never been to England to comprehend. The same goes for Proust and the French social scene, though I was struck by his insights and near-essays in *Remembrance of Things Past.* Eliot I thought a genius, with the added virtue of a sense of humour.

Around sixteen, I read more and more of Dostoyevsky and Conrad. At last I had decided what I liked and preferred. There was also Henry James in this period, an American-born writer, bridging the gap between American and English cultures. Adolescence was also the period of a thin but persistent interest in the metaphysical and religious: Hölderlin, Jakob Boehme, Christ, Sir Thomas Browne, Mary Baker Eddy. One knows that it is all true, somehow. It is the more certain when one attaches it to a living person, as I did in the form of a young photographer whom I met when I was twenty-one. He spoke like Christ and John Donne, and for six weeks I was dazzled, or in love, as one falls in love with the Church or with Christ. While still twenty-one, I awakened from this dream. I felt that Christ was the most beautiful of prophets, and that he was perhaps the most ambiguous. His words are few, and hardly a half of his counselling can be practised by the part of the world that has embraced the faith. It seemed to me that Christianity for the West is a guilt-builder, and this still seems to me its stranglehold.

Random books that I have liked and like: Graham Greene's *Brighton Rock,* Saul Bellow's *The Victim,* Italo Svevo's *Confessions of Zeno.* And I like biographies. Nelson, Conrad and Dostoyevsky are my heroes. I am perhaps naive. I like to read about people who have overcome great odds and have achieved something in life.

These days I'm often bored by current novels, especially the kitchen-sink, a-lay-a-page variety. I start novels sometimes and don't get beyond page twenty. I like books on zoology, evolution, sociology and social planning. An interesting book I read lately is Dennis Gabor's *The Mature Society,* a rather utopian book concerned with which strata of the society to educate, with the use of computers and the consequent need to learn how to spend leisure. What bores me most are family sagas, and long tales by women about shipwrecked marriages and love affairs. I have just ordered Erich Fromm's *The Anatomy of Human Destructiveness*. It is an attempt to explain sadism, so alive and well and living everywhere.

Writers I like at the moment are Iris Murdoch and Kingsley Amis. And in non-fiction, I like the books of Arthur Koestler always, because he is trying to push farther the frontiers of man's imagination, and trying also to chart the territories of intelligence and consciousness. This is another form of adventure, with new seas and continents to explore.

Is there something missing from this haphazard batch of books? Maybe mystery and detective stories. Apart from Sherlock Holmes and Edgar Allan Poe, I've never cared for them.

DAVID HOLBROOK

Reading and Discrimination

When I reflect on what books may have influenced me, when I was a child and adolescent, what I find emerging from memory are tactile experiences—I am on the stage of the Maddermarket Theatre, in Norwich, having my feet 'washed' by Christ as an Apostle at the Last Supper: I am searching the 'Latest Additions' shelf of Norwich City Library; I am fighting my way out of a cinema showing *Dante's Inferno*; I am sitting in the little wooden shed that served as a lavatory on a Norfolk farm, covered with honeysuckle, but otherwise somewhat basic, reading *Ulysses*, half the morning, as the sparrows cheeped outside.

My mother named me after David Copperfield, which book she adored, because Peggoty was such a good man, and reminded her of her own father, who was a wheelwright at Cromer in Norfolk. Actually, come to think of it, he couldn't have been all that good, because he drank away the family fortunes and left my grandmother to destitution. They lived on a sack of potatoes for a fortnight, until the mother managed to set up a boarding house, to keep her family. So, there must have been something sentimental in my mother's admiration for men like Peggoty. Certainly, however, in my child mind, was impressed strongly the Dickensian example—that literature was a vehicle for moral discrimination, between Steerforths and Peggoties, and that creative works delineated the progress of growth in protagonists, from innocence to experience, through sorrows and disappointments, towards fulfilment. *Pilgrim's Progress* was also part of my childhood reading, under my mother's influence. In my own work I am sure I am still influenced by the *David Copperfield* example, and while this perhaps gives me too assertive a belief that 'the essential function of art is moral', I am pleased to aspire to the Dickensian outlook. Who, in our century, can we put beside Dickens, for warmth and humanity, and a deep and genuine belief in people? And a concern to uphold humaneness against utilitarianism and the reduction of man to an object of contempt and exploitation? I have always loved Dickens, and have returned to him again and again, not least during the years when he was 'out' in the circles of high critical discrimination, until F. R. Leavis restored him to serious consideration. Today I believe Dr Roger Poole's essay on Leavis's work on Dickens ('Life Versus Death in the Later Criticism of F. R. Leavis', *Renaissance and Modern Studies,* Vol XVI, 1972, p. 112) is a locus classicus, an important statement in the debate on the way things are going. In this essay he shows that both Leavis and Dickens were existentialists, in the sense that what they are concerned with is: 'Where *is* that "life" which answers to our desire for "significance" to come from? What can we point to as living thought? Who is at the helm, who is responsible for "ends" and "significance"?' This has been my cultural concern, ever since the sixth form, until now.

My mother's love of Dickens, I believe, was also a link with the cultural tastes of the ordinary people in my childhood, as was my parents' respect for the Authorized Version of the Bible. Over this my father, whose cultural level was really represented by his addiction to the *Daily Express,* became grave and even poetic—a sharp contrast to his extraordinary behaviour at The Nest, Norwich City Football Ground, where, oblivious of his small son lost under the feet of the crowd, he would leap and dance hysterically, shouting sadistic obscenities about how the opposing team, and the referee, should be treated.

That there was another and less palatable side to human reality became apparent to me very early, as I crawled about on the floor, examining the books in the bookcase under the chiffonier. There was Apollyon towering over Pilgrim; and there was *Foxe's Book of Martyrs* in which there was an engraving of a man cutting off a naked woman's breast with a pair of shears apparently designed for the purpose. In our copy of the *History of Troy* there were illustrations in terracotta colour, many showing naked men impaled on spears. Burrowing through Dickens, I was terribly disturbed by the story of Gabriel Grubb, and Cruikshank's drawing of the demon leering with his long tongue haunted me in my nightmares for months. Yet, of course, whenever I was ill I had to read that horrible story again, out of a kind of compulsion, and would wake sweating in the night playing leapfrog over gravestones to escape the hideous gnome. But this kind of drug use of books goes with that mass of insignificant reading one does as a child—the *Magnet*, Jeffrey Farnol, murder stories, the *Children's Encyclopaedia*.

I think perhaps my concern about cultural rape springs from my experience as a child of eight of a film called *Dante's Inferno*. I can't think how my parents could have been so foolish as to take an infant to such a film, unless they thought I would benefit from a spectacle of Hell. The writhing masses of tortured people, suffering appalling punishments, reduced me to screaming hysteria, and they had to carry me out. They should have known how much I would respond, as I had reduced another cinema audience to hysterics, in quite another way, on a previous occasion, by my loud childish remarks on Charlie Chaplin in *Shoulder Arms*. I can still feel the suffocating horror some films induced in me as a child—one, for instance, in which some trapped miners hammered desperately on a pipe:

I thought I was going to die of fear. For people to say, today, that violent films have no effect seems to me to be the greatest hypocrisy. And the same applies to books: there are films and books which, in my adolescence, generated in me tormented hours, in which I would wonder, obsessively, whether life was worth living, and whether man was so vile as to make all effort hopeless. And this was before writers like Genet, Beckett, Mailer, David Storey and Edward Bond were available: it was my response to the worst Edgar Wallace and space fiction could do (I can't remember the name of a terrifying book about a death ray obliterating the world).

But there was, of course, another side to cultural influences. In my childhood this was represented by two major influences —a crazy English master, and the Maddermarket Theatre. Lance Harris, the English master, used to come in by train from Wroxham to Norwich and was often late. He would eat bananas behind his desk-lid, and shave himself during the first period sometimes, and then perhaps read us something from *Anna Livia Plurabelle*, E. M. Forster or T. S. Eliot in a booming voice. He ordered everything that was avant-garde, and we were writing pastiches of *Prufrock* or James Joyce at the age of fourteen. He would ask us to write chapters of novels, reportage, and poetry. If we wrote, as I did in those days, in the sentimental essayist style, or that of the local newspaper, our attempts would come back marked 'Drivel' or 'How can you write such insincere rubbish?' or 'See me!'. 'You have no aesthesis!' he would declare. Between this eccentric's lessons and the 'recent additions' shelf of the City Library we read our way through the Faber Renaissance, *Letters from Iceland*, *The Dog Beneath the Skin*, Lorca's poetry, Herbert Read on *Surrealism*, Hemingway's *For Whom the Bell Tolls*, books about Spain, and the exciting range of political books being published in those days—by Sir Norman Angell, George Orwell, Auden and Spender, and those of the Leavis-*Scrutiny* group in Cambridge. Another master at school, Andrew Wilkinson, introduced us to *Reading and Discrimination* and *Culture and*

Environment, and we would write for him pastiches of newspaper accounts of the bombing of Finland, the *Daily Worker* presenting it as a Good (or necessary) Thing and the *News Chronicle* as a Bad one. This teacher also introduced us to the pleasantly grave novels of Adrian Bell, which are so human, about joy, sex, and death.

Certainly, I believe, the atmosphere of the Sixth Form at an ordinary state school like mine was much more exciting then than today. We argued about politics all the time, and about culture, pacificism, music, sex, modes of living. I was reading Baudelaire, and books about artists like *Lust for Life*, a novel about Van Gogh. I wanted a mulatto mistress, and to be an artist, defying all conventions. Several of us did paint, and two boys from the school in fact went out actually to live by painting—one of them Michael Andrews, who is now both well-known and creatively successful as a painter. Our headmaster also painted, and would sometimes ask our opinion on how to finish a painting, which would cause great embarrassment if it faced us with a large pink lady in anatomical detail. We young boys desperately wanted to see nude ladies, but knew we would faint if we actually saw one. How to *finish* a painting of one we'd never know—though we all loved 'September Morn' in the illustrated book in the school library.

The Head, Geoffrey Thorp, sent us all down to the Maddermarket Theatre at fourteen, to help Nugent Monck, the owner and producer, to sweep up the bus-tickets and to hang curtains. Here literature came alive. We learned all the Shakespeare plays we worked in by heart, at rehearsals, and we handled real Elizabethan swords, clothes, and musical instruments. Monck's house was full of books, and had been visited by Shaw, Yeats, and others. Coming back from the theatre, to help Monck make a meal, after painting a set, one had to encounter 'famous' people, from the B.B.C. or the world of music, so that as a callow small-town youth one had quickly to acquire some kind of manners and conversation. Since this was nearly all about theatre and books, one had to do some reading to catch up. In one lunch-time I might be presented with the names of Monteverdi, the *commedia dell'arte,* Allardyce Nicoll, Pirandello, Stephen Spender, Verdi and Sartre—and at home I would sit up in my bedroom getting myself round these figures before the next working Saturday in the theatre.

It was one thing reading in a tiny bedroom in a small semi in a suburb: quite another sitting in the library of an Elizabethan house with someone playing a spinet downstairs, reading Dover Wilson or T. S. Eliot, while Moncklet was sitting in his armchair, stroking his bald head, trying to cut *Hamlet* for his forthcoming production. Was Ophelia pregnant? Did Hamlet overhear the King and Polonius taking their place to spy on him? How much of the bawdiness could a Norwich audience take? Monck's best customers were the lady and gentleman who owned the fish and chip shop on the corner of the next street—and he thought of them in planning his productions. At the Maddermarket I met some of the most charming and delightful people in education and other cultural pursuits in Norfolk between 1938 and 1945, many of them doctors and other professional workers in social services. To them the theatre was an almost sacred institution—but yet one which yielded an immense satisfaction and often joy to those taking part in it. Monck was a great artist, who could bring literature to life: he was perhaps the first to produce a mediaeval mystery play with a real Christ on the stage. This production reduced clergymen to hopeless weeping, and the atmosphere in the little theatre during the play was deeply moving, so immediate was the living story of the 'N' Town Mediaeval dramatist.

Monck would have nothing blasphemous and nothing lewd in his theatre: though, of course, there was always plenty that was genuinely bawdy, ironic, and even erotic. We used to perform in the open air at country houses and sometimes changed in the bushes, totally without inhibition. I was always in love with the current Juliet, or Beatrice, or whatever, and my knowledge of 'the world', of courtesanship, of lust, of sexual intrigue, advanced enormously throughout this period. Monck, who was a homosexual, had himself been a male prostitute, and his fund of information about the sexual antics of human beings was inexhaustible. When we got home from the theatre there would nearly always be couples copulating against the fence in Ninham's Court ('I must remember to go and pick up the French letters before Mrs Williamson comes to coffee') and we were ourselves as youths always trying to lure girls to firewatch with us at the theatre. But Monck made a powerful distinction, which has influenced me all my life, between the creative exploration of human love and lust—and that coarse kind of titillation that reduces literature, film or theatre to the level of a brothel. He knew the prostitutes who operated from the slums at the end of his alley, and would often help such people, if they were in trouble with the law. But, he said, 'neither my theatre nor my house are to become a brothel'—and I cannot imagine the depth of his distress as an artist, over what is happening today in the theatre, if he were alive.

After a year at Cambridge I went into the tanks, to return to Cambridge in 1945. Of course the main influence at this time was F. R. Leavis, who was my supervisor. My horizon now expanded to include George Eliot, Conrad, *What Maisie Knew, Wuthering Heights,* the other Metaphysicals than Donne and Herbert; Keats; Matthew Arnold, and, of course, D.H. Lawrence. One of the strangest aspects of the period just before this, 1941–2, was that we read with intensity books and poetry about the 14–18 war: Graves, Blunden, Edward Thomas, Wilfrid Owen, and to these Leavis himself added Rosenberg, who was not well known then. Monck had been in the trenches as a medical orderly, and told a funny story about trying to get rid of two amputated legs in the barrack-room stove: the sergeant nearly died, when, coming in drunk, he saw two legs partially sticking out of the coke stove. Our headmaster had been badly wounded, and was chucked out by the City Fathers for producing pacifists. Leavis himself had been in the 14–18 war, and spoke of his battered copy of *Paradise Lost*, which he had all the time in his knapsack. We took in from these men the misery now to be experienced by us in our turn, and we would sit reading these war poets as the first aeroplanes came streaking over our playing field to drop bombs on factories down at Trowse. *Goodbye to All That*, for this reason, was one of the books which has most impressed me—though we also read Sassoon, Barbusse and Remarque.

After all this misery, of the war and its shocks, what seemed important to me was that literature, and those critical works, which illuminated the problem of human hate. By contrast, I clung to those works which suggested by implication that imagination, vision, and the processes of love were central to human existence. Of these there were many: Leavis's own works like *Revaluation*; *The Road to Xanadu* by Livingstone Lowes, which gave me a life-long interest in Coleridge; *Illusion and Reality*, by Christopher Caudwell, which suggested the political importance of symbolism and the poetic; and *Seven Types of Ambiguity* by William Empson, which pointed to the complexity of poetic language, and to metaphorical richness in the English language.

I read a great deal of politics at this stage. But apart from Plekanhov's *The Role of the Individual in History* there was little that recognized those central issues of action and choice with which one was preoccupied. Moreover, even in works like George Thomson's *Marxism and Poetry*, there seemed too little recognition of the dynamics of consciousness and of symbolism: of metaphor and the subjective truths it explores.

The nature of metaphor, of course, was a central issue of Leavis's teaching, and this has led me in the years since to explore more and more the nature of subjective reality. This has led me in the end to find existentialist thought the most valid and creative approach to human life. I was very interested recently to see a reference in a lecture by Leavis to *The Knower and the Known* by Marjorie Grene. This philosopher, a follower of Michael Polanyi, is asking for a complete re-consideration of our philosophical paradigms, in the recognition that since Kepler, Galileo, Newton, Bacon and the seventeenth century we have been imprisoned in a limited 'objectivity', in Cartesian dualism, and in what Blake called 'Newton's sleep'. Like many undergraduates, I have felt that this in a vague way since reading Blake at the University, and listening to Basil Willey (*The Seventeenth-Century Background*). But to become explicitly conscious of the problem takes many years—and I have been led to it through the work of Leavis himself, L. C. Knights, and more recently *Towards Deep Subjectivity* by Roger Poole; *Where the Wasteland Ends,* by Theodore Roszak; *The Cult of the Fact* by Liam Hudson; and *Approaches to a Philosophical Biology*, by Marjorie Grene.

One of the most disturbing experiences I had as a boy of seventeen was seeing a play by Sartre, *Huis Clos,* put on with Beatrix Lehmann, and enthusiastically supported by the left-wing 'People's Convention' of those days (1940). I was appalled by the work, because of its hatred of human beings, and its nihilistic picture of the inevitable frustration of inter-human relationship and love. I have loathed Sartre ever since, and I still find it hard to understand how his love-denying nihilism became the main focus of avant-garde culture, and of the Left. Today, I believe, I can unravel the unrealities in Sartre—for certain major human experiences such as love, concern, and 'creative reflection' between people obviously mean nothing to him. He is blind and perverse. His elevation of Genet to a high status, and his obsession with perversion, have become the curse of Western literature and the stage. The effect, as Marcel argues (*A Philosophy of Being*), has been to reduce our concepts of man and his potentialities. Of course, there is a kind of heroism in Sartre: he sees man's 'thrownness' and he urges us to make our own choices and thus define ourselves. But there is something disastrous about the way in which in England and Europe Sartre has become the introduction to existentialism, while this philosophy means to most people his nihilistic brand. The whole strand of positive existentialism, delineated in Rollo May's introductory chapters in *Existence—A New Dimension in Psychiatry*, is virtually unknown to most people. Yet it is a substantial movement, beginning with Husserl, Bretano, Binswanger, and others associated with the work of Martin Buber, Tillich, Marcel and Merleau-Ponty. Paul Foulquié's *Existentialism* is perhaps the best introduction to this new existentialism. In psychotherapy some of the best writers are Viktor Frankl, as in *The Doctor and the Soul*; E. K. Ledermann in *Existential Neurosis*; Rollo May's *Love and Will*; Leslie Farber's *The Ways of the Will*, and Peter Lomas, *True and False Experience*.

What this positive existentialist movement lacks, of course, is a body of literature such as that created at the tail end of French nihilism, by Sartre and his followers. Moreover, Western literature has now become so saturated with moral inversion and implicit nihilism that it seems almost impossible for it to escape from a brutalism which has become immanent. Masud Khan argues, in a new essay on Camus (in *The Black Rainbow*, edited by Peter Abbs) that Western consciousness has to some extent become imprisoned in a new sensualistic mentalization of instinct, rather like the Outsider in his predicament in Camus's novel of that name. He lives for the moment, and he cannot connect his present actions with any past, or any meaning. The only thing that is real to him is death, and this implies a suicidal impulse, in Western consciousness itself—such as I have analyzed myself in Sylvia Plath. For this reason, it seems more urgent than ever to find our way out of this nihilistic *Huis Clos*.

My own critical concern arises from my experience as a youth, of being plunged into the experience of mass human hate, in the war. I tried to record this experience in *Flesh Wounds*, and, of course, it was a continual theme of our reading as students, and our discussions with older men—Leavis, Edgell Rickword, Herbert Read, Orwell—everyone we respected had suffered in war. I therefore decided that such talents as I had should be devoted to the investigation of human hate, and the moral inversions which generated it.

Human Hope and the Death Instinct was one of the books to come out of this determination. I felt that in all our critical work and creative preoccupations we were making assumptions about man's nature. But as I read books like D. W. Winnicott's *Collected Papers,* about his work with children, or Melanie Klein's *Narrative of a Child Analysis*—and certainly books like Marlon Milner's *On Being Able to Paint* and *In the Hands of the Living God*, the prevalent 'model' of human nature could not be sustained in the light of such insights. There is a certain Freudian model which underlies much of our thinking according to which man has, as it were, a certain quantity of libido, and a certain quantity of aggression, or even of death-impulse, to deal with. This may either be sublimated or, if it is repressed, it will burst out, inevitably, in dire displays of destruction. This basic 'brutal' model of man was one I could never accept—perhaps because of my grounding in Dickens, perhaps because I knew from experience that there was something much more creative in human beings. Work with children in school made one feel that the Winnicotts were right, and the Naked-Ape school wrong.

Here Ian Suttie's *The Origins of Love and Hate*—recommended, again, by the *Scrutiny* movement—was a turning point. In *Human Hope* I discuss Suttie, and relate his work to that of Melanie Klein, Freud himself, Winnicott and W. R. D. Fairbairn (author of *Psychoanalytical Studies of the Personality*). All these move, in their thought, towards a new model of man. According to them his central problem is his own sense of possible emptiness and meaninglessness. His primary problem is finding his human identity: here, in literature, Dostoyevsky's *Crime and Punishment* is a central work. In this work, Raskolnikov needs to act out the most dreadful attack on 'the other', in order to discover whether he is vermin or a human being. What he discovers is the capacity for concern—and love. This too is the path of other writers who have concerned themselves with *les bas fonds*—such as Gorki, who investigated the worst evils in order to sift from them the human grain of the capacity for love. Gorki's account of the birth of a human child in his autobiography was one of the great moments of my reading experience—enhanced by the marvellous film of the same episode. How can one read Gorki and believe that man's primary nature is brutish?

Very wide reading of psychoanalytical literature between 1955 and today has confirmed my original impression, when I felt such rejection of Sartre's *Huis Clos*, and his novels. The 'black' and nihilistic stream in Western literature since, although it takes itself as 'realistic', in fact depends upon distortions and lies. It belongs to the same reductionism which thinkers like Ernst Cassirer and Marjorie Grene are combating—thinking which belongs to elementary natural science of the nineteenth century, running quite contrary to the attitude to man of those who, like Blake, Dickens and F. R. Leavis, emphasize the creative, 'inward' and visionary qualities of man. In recent decades I have been unable to read much of contemporary literature. I find the destructive cynicism of a Kingsley Amis intolerable. I cannot read the kitchen-sink school who reduce man to such a square-fingered lecher, and women to such foul-mouthed judies. I cannot bear to think of the debasements of man, and especially of women, that take place nightly on the London stage, while the cinema has become for me a nightmare of dehumanization. I am appalled to find such trivial lewdness being offered as worthy of attention, in the novels of intellectuals like Iris Murdoch: one only has to compare her prose with that of, say, Dickens, or Solzhenitsyn, say, to see that the English sensibility has shrunk to a small and withered sickness, like a plant attacked by some malignant infection. It displays a fundamental death of interest in and concern for the human soul. Indeed, reading Solzhenitsyn's work recently has been for me a major experience. I had begun to feel that perhaps the fault was in me, that I could find no warm, human and gravely serious celebration of man's value. Strangely enough, I find something of this now in Patrick White, as in *The Vivisector*, despite his obsession with bodily nastiness and his evident hatred of human beings. But in Solzhenitsyn there is a capacity to uphold the dignity and value of man, his capacity for love and creativity, even in the most impossible and sordid circumstances, which we in the West seem to have lost completely, under the influence of Sartre and the schizoid nihilists who have followed him into the black realms of violence, under the excuse that this is 'man re-creating himself'. I believe, rather, that the effect of the literature of violence and the obscene in the West has led to a situation in which man is *unmaking* himself. We are being plunged back into the old degeneracies, even in the name of freedom and 'enlightenment'. A clue to the underlying processes is given by Rollo May in his latest book, *Power and Innocence,* in which he analyzes both violence and obscenity as manifestations of impotence. Harry Guntrip, whose book *Personality Structure and Human Interaction* was important in my explorations of psychoanalysis, says much the same: 'It is the weak who hate: only the strong can love.' The frenetic destructiveness of our literature today is a mark of a failure to have anything to say. (Strangely enough, one of the best books to make this point is Iris Murdoch's study of Sartre!)

This, alas, is my final judgment on D. H. Lawrence, who is a major influence on me. Lawrence has marvellous things to say about existence in *Sons and Lovers*, and in *The Rainbow*: and, especially, in some of the best short stories—like *Odour of Chrysanthemums*. But in recent years I have come more and more to believe that Lawrence has contributed a great deal to the sickness of our culture itself. F. R. Leavis, I fear, draws a discreet screen over the sodomy in *Lady Chatterley*, and its meaning—that woman must be exorcized of all the deadly peril that lurks in her body. This impulse, which lies, of course, behind pornography, is given free rein in the 'demented fantasies', as Kate Millett calls them, of his last works—*The Woman Who Rode Away*, and *The Plumed Serpent,* in which woman is subjected to the 'death fuck'. One may find the same sick and nihilistic impulses in the poems *Look! We Have Come Through!* I find today that a deep disturbance comes over me when I realize that young men are trying to work out their love affairs on the basis of Lawrence's sick advice, which is, for one thing, that sexual problems are best worked on by sensual effort, of a rather cruel kind, with a good deal in it of trying to humiliate and break the woman's power (her 'beak-like clitoris'!). I also feel despair when I realize that the fact that they are watching sodomy on the cinema screen, before coming to read John Donne—and that this virtually prevents them from fully responding to his poetry—is due to Lawrence's obsession with the functions and organs of sex; and, of course, his verbal treadmill, and his need for explicitness, where tacit awareness would have served us much better.

As a taxi-driver said to me recently, over *Last Tango*, 'They're hoping for something new.' We all knew about these things, years ago. I remember, sitting on that farm bumby in Reepham, working my way through Molly Bloom's soliloquy and various other books like Rabelais and a German history of pornography. But what interested me most about *Ulysses* was Bloom's alienation from his wife, and Stephen's alienation from his country: and then the attempt of each to weave the other into a relationship that made up for things they had never experienced: chiefly love. Pornography and bawdiness seemed then to belong to a fringe aggressiveness that seemed sometimes politically useful, and sometimes important to a few odd creatures. The disaster that has happened since has been in the success with which foolish intellectuals have brought these forms of aggression to the centre of the stage, and the way in which commerce has forced them into every corner of the kingdom—to the exclusion of much else, and with the effect of virtually drowning the warm-hearted, loving, caring element such as we find in Dickens. For many, I believe, far more than we realize, this means virtually the end of the novel, of film, and of the theatre—even (after *Crow*) of poetry. The absurdity of intellectuals, for instance, admiring and acclaiming the primitive, commercially-angled, brutal fantasies of Ian Fleming, seemed to me a major moment of treachery in English intel-

7

lectual history—about which I have written in *The Masks of Hate* (for which their revenge has been to refuse to review it).

Ever since reading the work of Leavis and Thompson, and that of Wildrid Mellers in music, (*Man and His Music*), I have felt that one's good luck, in being given scholarships and exhibitions, and the enriching experiences of literature such as the Maddermarket gave me, obliged one to do what one could with one's gifts, to contribute to the life of the community. I believe that knowledge brings responsibilities, as Marjorie Grene emphasizes. All the men who have influenced me, like Leavis, Henry Morris (who invented the village colleges) and Nugent Monck, have all been poor men. Morris and Monck died leaving nothing. Yet they made thousands happier.

By contrast, the 'progressive' pornographers of our time, and those who have worked deep veins of hate in their writing, have made fortunes. Today I share the Marxist attitude to this: culture has become sunk in exploitation. Everything I have read which I have respected and admired makes this kind of prostitution a serious betrayal of cultural trust and of meaning. This, to me, in the light of serious philosophical studies, such as those of Susanne Langer, is the worst that man can do to man. If, as she says, 'Bad art is corruption of feeling' (*Philosophical Sketches*), then the central issue in our culture is to resist and oppose the corruption of man's central need, the pursuit of meaning.

In my youth one used to be able to look along that shelf of new books and find marvellous new human products—like Louis MacNeice's translation of the *Aeschylus of Agamemnon*, or a book on the Bauhaus, or a Mass-Observation study of the lives of ordinary people and their institutions. Today, I fear, I would approach such a 'recent additions' shelf with trepidation, and a readiness to avoid pain by trying not to see the offensiveness displayed there—to so many acts of menticide and treachery, as Joost de Meerlo has called them.

ELIZABETH JANE HOWARD

I didn't start off very well. Earliest memory of a book is sitting on the floor aged about three and a half and tearing each glossy page of *Mrs Tiggy Winkle* in half. I did not like her prickles sticking through her clothes, but I enjoyed the slow, luxurious tearing of the art paper. I couldn't read until I was six, so I used to pretend: taking a large dark-coloured book off the shelf, sitting in an armchair and turning the pages at what I believed to be appropriate intervals. When I was seven, my younger brother wrote a book called *Percy Rainsbull Edwards The Adventures of a Pig*. I thought he was simply too childish not to know that writing a book meant taking a book off a shelf and copying it in one's best writing, and largely to show everybody that I knew this, partly not to be outdone by a whippersnapper of five, I set about it. The book I chose was *Happy Families*, and I soon got bored with the task, while my brother wrote and finished his book in a state of mounting excitement and fear (Percy's life was a dangerous one involving a trip to Africa where there were monkeys and snaks [*sic*]. From the age of seven I read pretty well whatever I could lay hands on. As this was nothing like enough, I re-read a great deal, and by the time I was nine began writing a book simply in order to have more to read:

the book was the life story of a horse and incredibly dull. Favourite re-reads were E. Nesbitt, L. M. Alcott, Anna Sewell, Ernest Thompson-Seton and all the Andrew Lang fairy books that an uncle gave me every year for Christmas. I also very much enjoyed books about being wrecked on a desert island —Marriot, Ballantyne and so on—as I regarded this hazard as a desirable likelihood the moment I started to travel, and wanted to be properly prepared for it. For years my favourite fantasy was an endless saga about such an adventure: there was a piece of red colour on my blue paisley eiderdown that *was* the island and set me off at once and in the end I had a house, a raft for fishing, a garden, animals and some children —acquired by the casual process of imagining them.

I was nine when I first encountered Shakespeare, who was an instant hit, and I contemplated the long row of volumes that belonged to my mother with satisfaction. I had reached the age when if I liked any writer I wanted them to have written a great many books: to know that there was a good store of sure-fire reading ahead, before I had to find someone new who then might turn out to be no good. I was twelve before I had saved up enough money to buy a complete edition of my own (O.U.P. Complete Works, ten bob). I got the money for ironing my father's trousers at threepence a pair, but this took time, as it was forty pairs of trousers, and although I had sixpence a week for pocket money, that went on a number of other things, like goldfish, mice, and, saving for four weeks—a terrible strain—an Everyman Dickens at two shillings. Jane Austen, another instant winner, was in the house, but it was a long time before I actually owned her novels. Meanwhile, I remember reading *The Painted Veil* stealthily, having been told that it was unsuitable, so I had to keep taking it out for a short, guilty read, and putting it back again before anyone noticed. I also got hold of a translated Chinese novel called *Chin Ping Mei* (I think) that belonged to a godfather who stayed some time with us. It was almost entirely about sex, and understanding not more than a third of it, I still enjoyed the book—largely because I was deeply enamoured of everything Chinese. Pearl Buck and the great Chinese Exhibition in the 'thirties had started me off, so although a bit bored by the sex (I was not precocious in this respect) I was fascinated by Chinese customs, food, clothes, conversation and life generally.

Shakespeare I read aloud every day at home—where I was taught—and I learned thirty lines a week by heart. I also read every book I could lay hands on about the First World War, and the more I read, the more frightened I became at the prospect of another, even worse war. Guy Chapman's anthology *Vain Glory* I remember particularly informed my fears, but there were some jollier, more simply adventurous books about our ace submariners. All these books were re-read: by this time I was reading all of Jane Austen every year, in fact, I remember reading as a principal occupation. The reading went on everywhere: on buses, up apple trees during the holidays, in bed with a torch after hours, during meals unless prevented, and particularly, in a huge, battered armchair, like a leather cell, which exactly fitted me. This was followed at some distance by writing. The horse book plodded on—to reach a record dreary 400 pages, by which time it had palled, even on me. But I also wrote a number of stories, mostly of a satirical nature, a certain amount of verse, and two plays. I had no thought of being a writer of any kind, having early determined that acting and the theatre was to be my life. By now I was reading a certain number of books *about* Shakespeare: Dover Wilson, Quiller-Couch, Masefield, Mackail—even Rosamund Gilder on Gielgud's *performance* of Hamlet. Looking back on it, I have little idea now how much I understood of what I read then: I had become accustomed to not understanding everything, and did not in the least mind it. The result was that the re-readings were usually illuminating; every time I re-read a book, something new became clear. It is this experience that makes me sure that writing down to children is not necessary: if the book is a good one, the young reader can get a charge out of it without necessarily having total grasp of everything that the author is on about. I read more poetry—entirely because of Shakespeare, but I found that when it was good (I mean by that only that it impressed me), it was rather like living on neat brandy as opposed to the wine and beer and (too often) orange squash of prose. A little went a long way. I cried copiously, and that too, was a pleasure. Marlowe, Ben Jonson, Donne came in here; the first two largely because they had written plays. About this time, Penguin Books began, and with them, the welcome prospect of being able to buy a book a week. Unfortunately their production (at that stage) did not keep up with my pocket money. I would read about Mustapha Kemal and Shelley, and then there would be an uneasy pause. I was still after value for money before almost anything else. In Church Street, where second-hand books lay on the pavement outside junk shops, I once picked up two handsome leather-bound volumes for a penny. The work was called *Coelebs in Search of a Wife*. It seemed intoxicating value and I read it because I had bought it. I read a great deal of the time, but suffered (looking back on it) from a great deal of ignorance coupled with lack of curiosity. Why, for instance, did I never encounter George Eliot until I was over twenty? And Blake? And Stendhal? It points to weaknesses of character so profound that whatever I think about them by now they cannot be wholly eradicated. I *did* try a certain number of novelists (probably too young) who failed me at the first attempt, and with some I have never tried again. Conrad, Meredith, Trollope, Hardy, Stevenson and Thackeray come to mind. The last three have a limited attraction for me now after further essays, the others have remained closed books. By the time I was sixteen, I had read hundreds of plays (it was how I first encountered Turgenev), and had begun to read contemporary poetry for the first time. Turgenev led me to some other Russians—notably Tolstoy and Dostoyevsky. When I was seventeen I thought that E. M. Forster was marvellous.

By now it was the Second World War: I was working and writing a good deal and my reading—random as ever—took third place. Wells, Butler, John Stuart Mill, Mary Shelley, Norman Douglas, Hemingway (when I was eighteen I thought Hemingway was stunning), Graham Greene, Waugh, Flaubert, Ford Maddox Ford—at twenty-two I thought Ford was incredibly good—Virginia Woolf, Firbank, Rolfe ... I now discovered what a high proportion of men that I got to know wanted to educate me. List after list of reading matter was sternly or affectionately compiled: I did my best, but hadn't a hope of keeping up with it: the gaps in my knowledge were so many, so wide and so deep, that almost *anyone* could produce thirty books that I hadn't read. I spent months bogged down with early miracle plays, Chaucer, huge critical works about philosophers I had never read—sometimes the philosophers themselves—what a time I had with Spinoza for instance,—it was all a long way off from the carefree Penguin days. Good things came out of it. Eliot, Fielding and Richardson's *Clarissa*, which I have read twice and is one of the greatest novels I've ever read. I never thought Virginia Woolf was much good, although I tried harder with her than most, because so many people I loved and admired admired her. By now I had written four plays and was well into a novel—still without in the least meaning to become a writer. This really meant that I didn't—consciously, anyhow—relate my own writing to anybody else's, and the first and only time in my life when I came up against another writer was when I tried to read Proust—immediately thought that he was marvellous, but found that he totally paralyzed me from writing a line. It was an extraordinary feeling: I stopped instinctively, and a few weeks later began writing again. About ten years later, I tried to read him again, with exactly the same result. The first time this happened was when I knew that I wanted to go on trying to write. Proust was banned from reading lists.

Years later, and I have now read a certain number of books. The reading lists have dwindled away, not because I am now a well-read person, so much as that people have given up trying to educate me. I am back to the carefree days. Apart from a little reviewing, and the steady stream of typescripts that ambush one from absolutely anywhere by some of that frightening quantity of people who have found time to write a novel, I can read what I please. Since the war, the novelist who has impressed me most is Elizabeth Taylor, who never writes a bad book, is never pretentious, dishonest and therefore dull; who has the sense of proportion that combines humour with what Jane Austen describes as taste and we now call feeling, and whose manner is quiet, economical and apparently easy. I love clarity: I cannot stand writers who use characters merely as mouthpieces for their own opinion—a peculiarly self-indulgent and pernicious fault. I love irony, wit, humour, entertainment: a humourless writer is seldom any good to me. Using the term generically, humour is often the only accurate means of description: anything else proving coarser, duller and less telling. I hate 'poetic prose' as it is usually a euphemism for nonsense meant to be taken seriously because the words are so beautiful. I am tired of the people—and this includes writers—who claim that they cannot be bothered to read about certain areas of behaviour or society. If, as Norman Douglas remarked 'everything is worth talking about', then everything must be worth writing about: nothing is intrinsically wrong with any subject-matter, it all depends upon the manner in which it is done. Lack of humour, self-pity and priggishness are dangerously current faults in too many novelists. That, and a general sloppiness both of observation and of writing. Novels are for understanding and finding out about people; language is for making things plain; the more a novelist thinks it is important for the reader to understand exactly what he means, the more trouble he must take to express himself as simply as he can contrive. This is so much more difficult than most people—including some writers—think, that interesting simplicity is at a premium. So, I admire Elizabeth Taylor. I like Henry Green. I like some of

Carson McCullers. The two single novels that have impressed me most, I think, in the last ten years have been *The French Lieutenant's Woman* and *Watership Down.* John Fowles's novel because it has a romantic/moral quality that carries and keeps the reader inside his imagined and real world, and *Watership Down* because it evokes another dimension of life here and now. One cannot dismiss the first as merely Hardyesque, nor the second as merely a novel about rabbits from the rabbits' point of view.

I still love all of Shakespeare and all of Austen. I love Stendhal, Richardson's *Clarissa,* most of George Eliot, some Turgenev, Charlotte Brontë's *Villette,* Fielding, Tolstoy's *Anna Karenina,* Flaubert's *Madame Bovary*, Thackeray's *Vanity Fair, Bleak House, Great Expectations* and a great many other pieces of Dickens's novels. I could think of many single works that have touched or impressed me, but these are the main writers in my bloodstream. Sadly, there is not the slightest use in my making a reading list, because most people already know and have known for years what I now like.

EDWARD HYAMS

Maybe a writer shouldn't have read anything: I'm thinking of the well-known danger of deriving books from books instead of from life. Who was it that said, in answer to the question 'Have you read such-and-such?', 'I don't *read* books, I write 'em.'? On the other hand through other men's books you can live a hundred lives almost as digestible as your own.

As far as I can recall it was a story called *In Bunyip Land* followed by a book called *Hercules and the Marionettes* which first got me hooked on reading; though what I first wrote was very bad poetry. The Hercules of my first experience of the novel was a poor boy whose only property was a spoon-mould and some lead; he got his living by walking from town to town, selling lead spoons. Maybe he accounts for my brief flirtation with the picaresque.

No reading ever compared, for me, with the reading of novels; I mean, of course, reading for pleasure. Poetry has never made anything like the impression made by prose, and very early indeed came the pleasure of distinguishing between prose *written,* as the French say; and just prose.

My parents' bookcase had bound sets of Dickens, Thackeray and George Eliot; I went through the lot in my early 'teens, conceived a distaste for Dickens, was bored by Thackeray, and was left with George Eliot as a favourite for life. (I still place her first among English novelists.) But by then I had a taste for good bad books, and the first novelist I became addicted to was Nat Gould, who introduced me to the pleasures of story-telling below the level of the high morality or the socially significant; and of the kind of writing which isn't 'literature'—I deplore that distinction, but you know what I mean.

H. G. Wells started a lifelong taste for SF. My brother, four years younger, and I shared a bedroom and night after night I kept us awake with an off-the-cuff serial about our adventures in an airship; it was far in advance of its time. There was a romantic element to the story, but it was awkward; I mean, there had to be a girl and some sentiment but it was difficult to be sure what they were there for; derivative work, I'm afraid.

My reading in boyhood and youth went in periods. The first I can distinguish clearly was for the picaresque: *Tom Jones,* of course, *Gil Blas* (my first in French), and at last *Don Quixote*, which I've never been able to re-read; it's surely one of the most boring novels ever written. Then, romantic adventure, with Rider Haggard as the master; many years later I discovered from one of his essays that I shared that delight with Graham Greene.

My French period, as I now realize, began very early and it was, if I may be forgiven the pomposity, the most formative, as they say, though French literature was taken, like pills by a medicine addict, at random, romantics, realists, satirists all mixed up. For quite a long time it seemed to me that Anatole France was the world's greatest novelist; he's still on my shelves and I re-read *L'Ile des Pingouins* and *Les Dieux Ont Soif* from time to time. From the French I digressed into the Russians, read and re-read them, until I had sorted what I knew I ought to admire, Dostoyevsky for example, from what really made a lasting impression, Tolstoy and Lermontov; and from what became a lifelong addiction and was, presumably, really to my taste—Turgenev, and Pushkin as prose-writer.

I fancy that I was always, unconsciously, seeking a particular combination: the romantic story very dryly told, with the apparent simplicity produced by the subtle and elegant manipulation of language. If that be true, it's a marvel how long it took me to work my way through three literatures to my supreme novelist. I thought I had found that paragon in Jane Austen until, at last, I discovered Stendhal; and in his, alas small, body of work, that masterpiece (which, by the way, has never been even adequately translated), *Lucien Leuwen*. I knew then what I really delighted in: *writing*. I found that delight in a very wide range of authors in several literatures. Gibbon, for example, gave and gives me the pleasure others find in poetry. It's possible to laugh in sheer pleasure at some of his rhythms but a lot of my pleasure is in economy of means, that is in prose written as sparsely as poetry, if it's of the kind I can enjoy (e.g. Shakespeare's in his non-grand passages and vernacular exchanges). Gibbon can do you a character in eight words: (George of Cappadocia: 'His occupation was base; he rendered it infamous').

Looking for others who could work that enchanting miracle I found them, very late (having the wrong kind of education), in the classics. At the same time and on that other level I was reading a great deal of the kind of agreeable rubbish which never gets a place on the shelves: 'Sapper', and even—I have a debilitating streak of sentimentality, or used to have—Gene Stratton Porter, though chiefly because I was fascinated by the scenery and life of the Limberlost. I needed that help to get me through Virgil, than whom no other writer ever bored me more excepting Cervantes. In the end I rejected all the Latins excepting Catullus as not for me, and was left with five Greeks: Herodotus and Thucydides; a little of Plato; the sublime comedian Aristophanes; and Xenophon in two of his books —the *Anabasis* and, oddly enough, the *Oikonomikos*. During the Second World War, while at sea in a destroyer, I went back to the Greeks, I'm not sure why; and by using the Loeb edition, even taught myself some Greek.

As for travel writing, I've enjoyed very little of it and that little the most ancient, most remote, most, as it were, Sinbad-like. Marco Polo survives, and an odd little book from first-century Alexandria, *The Periplus of the Erythraean Sea*, though it contains nothing but bare bones useful to masters of merchantmen.

Discoveries followed by periods of addiction have marked my reader's progress. I had a year of nothing but Proust and go back to him, in selected passages, from time to time; he made me realize that, for me, writers reach their zenith in comedy, perhaps because it's *dans le vrai*, though I'd be hard put to it to defend the implication that tragedy isn't. Yet it took a love affair, and a late one at that, with an Irishwoman, to teach me to read the greatest of all comic novels, I mean *Ulysses*, despite the fact that I'd long since adopted *Dubliners*, and *A Portrait of the Artist as a Young Man*.

I believe it was the, as it were, habit of Proust which opened to me the extraordinary world of William Faulkner. I really began on the Americans in the early 'thirties, with Carl van Vechten and Scott Fitzgerald, have retained neither, and cannot re-read Hemingway; but Faulkner, like diamonds, is for ever.

The writer who revived my early relish for SF was Olaf Stapledon; odd that the critics of the *genre* seem to have forgotten *First and Last Men* and the rest, especially those SF curiosities *Odd John* and *Sirius*. The enjoyment of escaping into space and out of time is still there. I loved John Wyndham's huge catastrophes; and Hoyle because his scientists were always slapping down insolent politicians. Clarke and Asimov are the masters; I like some SF best described as 'gothic' but not the kind full of poetic whimsicality.

It's been interesting to try to identify my, as it were, permanents among contemporaries or near contemporaries:

Faulkner I've mentioned; there is all Camus, Evelyn Waugh, Richard Hughes, Patrick White and Grahame Green; Solzhenitsyn, Alejo Carpentier and Elias Canetti. And, at the spy/crime level, Dashiel Hammett, Patricia Highsmith, Simenon and John le Carré. A question arises: why have, at one level J.-P. Sartre, at the other the Sherlock Holmes stories, for both of which I had a passion, become unreadable?

Taking another quick glance over the shelves I find a large number of books often re-read which seem to have nothing in common excepting that one quality of being *written*. I can't list them all but here's a random sample: the two best biographies (to my mind) of our time—Nicolaev's *Vie de Karl Marx* and Rolt's *Isambard Kingdom Brunel; Alice in Wonderland;* my own translation of Hippolyte Taine's *Notes on England*; Edward Sackville-West's *The Sun in Capricorn*; some of Montaigne's *Essays*; *Rewards and Fairies* and *Puck of Pook's Hill; Tono-Bungay;* Miles Hadfield's *Gardening in Britain*; Georgina Masson's *Frederick von Hohenstauffen*; Prescott's *Conquest of Mexico* and *Conquest of Peru*; Helen Waddell's *Peter Abelard*; Hope Munz's *The Golden Warrior*; *Lark Rise to Candleford;* most of Robert Graves; Mommsen's *History of Rome* ...

It's been interesting to me to see what is there but not read any more, books which rouse no inclination to look at them again: Boswell's *Life of Doctor Johnson*; Rabelais, whom once I loved; the collections of plays—French, Spanish and Russian as well as English, but Shakespeare still the only one now ever read for pleasure. I've sometimes looked into one of the pure philosophers for my work, but haven't opened one of them from inclination for twenty years. I seem to enjoy history as it used to be written; but not as it is now.

What I have been reading for, for half a century? Say ten per cent for the pleasure of acquiring information; and ninety per cent for the unalloyed and incomparable delight of having a master of language tell me a story.

FRANCIS KING

Both in literature and in life, it is usually the first-class that provokes our deepest admiration but the second-class that exerts the strongest influence on us. Looking back over my life, I see that one of its most important decisions was my refusal, at the age of fifteen, to join the school Officer Training Corps (in those pre-war days it was inconceivable that any public school should train its boys for the Other Ranks), since from that decision stemmed my later decision to become a conscientious objector, and from that again stemmed my isolation in a remote Essex village and my efforts to relieve my acute loneliness by embarking on a novel. Yet what led me to the first of those decisions was a reading not of the New Testament, of Tolstoy, of Aldous Huxley or even of Middleton Murry but, of all people, of the creator of Winnie the Pooh. Later, when war had engulfed the world, A. A. Milne was to repudiate the pacifism advocated in his *Peace with Honour*; and, still a schoolboy, I then wrote to this Lost Leader a letter of ingenuously bitter reproach. The answer I received was impeccable in its courtesy and good sense—qualities conspicuously absent from my own tirade. Life, Milne explained, ought to be a perpetual process of learning; and if it were that, then it must also be a continual process of readjustment and revision. He was, of course, right: consistency is claimed as a virtue only by those who lack the will or the ability to learn—and by politicians. But at the time I felt cruelly betrayed.

At school I spent the major part of my working hours in studying Greek and Latin, since in those days that was what any boy who won a scholarship to Shrewsbury was expected to do. Had I received even the vestiges of a scientific education, I might have fulfilled my ambition to become a doctor; but a classical education led to a classical scholarship to Balliol and the academic tramlines carried me inexorably away from the direction in which I had really wished to travel.

From my study of Cicero, Tacitus, Caesar, Thucydides, Pliny and Plato, I learned to value what I still value highly in literature and life: lucidity. Here—especially in Plato—were often extremely complex and difficult things; but the manner in which they were expressed made them as clear as they could ever be.

But, oddly, the most profound influence that the Classics exerted on me was an indirect one: they forced me to make a microscopically close examination of passages of English poetry through the twin weekly tasks of producing Greek and Latin 'verses'. I remember well how, at the age of sixteen, I was struggling to twist and squeeze a section of Tennyson's *Ulysses* into Latin hexameters when all at once—it was as though a sudden shaft of brilliant sunshine had pierced a leaden, thundery sky—I realized that before me lay something more than just a heap of words and phrases to be wearisomely fitted together like the pieces of some diabolic jigsaw puzzle.

> ... Tho' much is taken, much abides; and tho'
> We are not now that strength which in old days
> Moved earth and heaven; that which we are, we are;
> One equal temper of heroic hearts,
> Made weak by time and fate, but strong in will
> To strive, to seek, to find, and not to yield.

I was at first stunned and then amazingly exhilarated by the wholly unexpected glory of it. Similar, previously wearisome, tasks kindled an abiding love for two other poets similarly now unfashionable: Matthew Arnold and A. E. Housman.

I think that, of the three, it was Housman who then moved me most, although now I inevitably acknowledge the narrowness of his range, the facility of his pessimism and his inferiority to the two Victorians. None the less he seems to me over and over again to equal his master Heine in the sardonic pathos of his verse. What a pity that there has been no Schubert but only Vaughan Williams and some other, minor English composers to set him to music! From Housman I took the title of one of my earliest novels, *An Air that Kills*. As a schoolboy I turned to him over and over again in moments of despair, deriving a curious comfort from a view of life even bleaker than my own. From time to time I still turn to him and I can still recite many of his poems with no need of prompting.

It was at school, too, that I first discovered Freud—reading first *The Psychopathology of Everyday Life* and then *Introductory Essays in Psychoanalysis*. I acknowledge now that Freud provides a number of examples in his own work of his theory of the unconscious suppression of disagreeable or unwelcome memory—obviously he was too honourable a man to have consciously lied and dissimulated; and I also now acknowledge the shakiness of the scientific premises on which many of his theories have been erected. But if, like the New Testament, much of his work approaches nearer to myth than to fact, the myth, like the Christian one, has never ceased to illuminate the darkest corners of existence for me. Freud reconciled me to much that was baffling in others and, more important, in myself; and if, with a personality as anomalous as my own, I have none the less contrived to have an almost continuously happy life along admittedly austerely narrow lines, I owe it largely to him. 'I'm not at all sure that this is really very suitable reading for you,' one of my masters said reprovingly when he found *The Psychopathology of Everyday Life* open on my desk.

He would probably have felt easier if he had caught me perusing *London Life* or *Men Only*; then at least he could have confiscated the matter without any hesitation.

Of modern novelists, the two who had most influence on me are Somerset Maugham and E. M. Forster—one a Class II Division I novelist, the other a Class I Division II novelist. From Maugham I learned more about the technique of fiction—of how to establish a character, of how to pace a narrative, above all, of how to make an effect with a minimum of preparation and fuss—than from anyone else. Unfortunately I acquired, too, by a process of osmosis, some of his cynical, world-weary view of the people around him and it was to be some years before I learned to survey the human comedy entirely through my own eyes. His actual style never impressed me, even in my early years, and I am always astonished when I read some critic of the fastidiousness of Cyril Connolly giving it praise. Impoverished, cliché-ridden and without rhythm or euphony, it contrasts dismally with the style of a little-known novelist whom I have always admired: Forrest Reid. Time and again Reid effortlessly achieves the combination of simplicity, lucidity and strength that eluded Maugham.

A friend of Forster, Reid produced the best of his novels out of an intense and (I should guess) sexually unfulfilled passion for young boys. The themes of his books have seldom held much interest for me; but the writing—so serene, so elegant, so precise, above all, so musical—has always struck me as some of the finest of this century.

Forster's influence was profound on me, as on most of the writers of my generation, and I revered him even more than I revered Somerset Maugham or Ivy Compton-Burnett. I always longed to meet him; but when I did so, I felt a heavy, chilling disappointment, the exact reverse of what I felt with both Ivy Compton-Burnett and Maugham, neither of whom I had expected to like. That disappointment was never wholly banished at subsequent meetings. I had expected neither a personality so formidable—alert, in a schoolmistressy way, for any errors of taste or judgment, for any vulgarity of style or soul—nor one so unobtrusively self-preening (though God knows there was ample in his achievement on which to preen himself!). I had spent my childhood in India, where my father, like his father before him, was one of those 'Burtons and Turtons' so derided by Forster. At a period of adolescent revolt I was deeply impressed by his seeming demolition of a ruling caste to which so many members of my father's and mother's families had belonged. Only now do I realize how unfair *A Passage to India* is in its picture of its almost uniformly philistine, snobbish and stupid Anglo-Indians (I use that term in its old sense, of English people working in India). At a period when the majority of those who passed out highest in the Civil Service examinations opted for India, there was no lack of brilliant linguists (like my father), remarkable conversationalists and men of wide and deep culture in remote stations all over the sub-continent. Sir Malcolm Darling, on whom Forster's Fielding is often said to be based, was by no means unique.

My five years on the land as a conscientious objector enabled me not merely to write but to read extensively, since in the evenings there was little else to do. It was then that I devoured all Dickens, all Thackeray, all George Eliot, all Jane Austen, all Fielding, all the Brontës, all Conrad. Now, when so much of my time has to be spent on reading the second-rate for review or the third-rate for publishers, it is wonderful to have that literarary capital stored away from those years. Of all those novelists it is Conrad who has most consistently fascinated me, making me go back again and again to *Under Western Eyes* (finer, in my unorthodox view, than *The Possessed*), *The Secret Agent*, *Victory*, *Romance*. (The sea-novels have always bored me in spite of the magnificence of their purple passages.) Whereas I can just imagine that by somehow stretching myself I might manage to produce a novel that would not disgrace Forster, I cannot ever conceive of myself producing a novel worthy of Conrad. He seems remoter from me, in his disdainfully aristocratic confrontation of life no less than in his imaginative grandeur, than any other English novelist of this century; and yet there is no other whose works I should rather have written.

Proust, another potent influence, came much later, at a period when I was lying ill in the Hospital of St John and St Elizabeth. I remember one of the nuns rustling in, peering to see what I was reading and then saying, in her curiously debby drawl, as she prepared the syringe, 'Oh, but you *must* read him in French! Whatever anyone says, he's much, much better in French.' Well, I never did. But on each occasion when I have had a long illness I have once again embarked on that vast, sinuous, powerful river. I have a friend who says that he has ceased to read *Emma*, because he wishes to keep it for when he is dying. I do not have to cease to re-read Proust; I know that over and over again he will continue to satisfy me, as will, in her totally different way, Ivy Compton-Burnett.

Gide was also once a passion; but now when I take him up again, it is as though I were going through a trunk containing the clothes that I wore as an undergraduate. Can that really have been my taste? Mann, on the other hand, exerts the same power, the incandescence of his genius blazing on through the faulty wiring of those abysmal Lowe-Porter translations. If only he had had the good fortune to find a Scott Moncrieff or a Dorothy Bussy!

My journeyings about the world for the British Council took me to Greece; and I was young enough and stayed there long enough to learn passable modern Greek. That, usually lazy about working at languages, I none the less made that effort, has meant that I have had the good fortune to read in his own tongue the poet whom I admire most of this century: Cavafy. As in the case of Housman, I immediately found something of myself in the Alexandrian's poems about transitory ecstasies, remembered love, regret for things said wrongly or not said at all, despair.

After Greece came Japan; and I was fortunate in being given by a friend, before I went East, two books that, unlike every other book that I have read before visiting a country, struck me on arrival as being absolutely correct in every important particular. One was Ruth Benedict's *The Chrysanthemum and the Sword*; the other D. J. Enright's *The World of Dew*. Japan is, perhaps, the only country about which it is both possible and permissible to generalize, since there is so little that is spontaneous and so much that is conventional in behaviour. But none the less it amazes me that of these two writers the American had never visited the country and the Englishman stayed there for little more than a year. If (as I like to think) I was quicker and more adept at unravelling the complexities of that strange, chilling country than many of my colleagues, and if I managed to make a large number of close Japanese friends, it was as much due to those two books as to the circumstance that I was alone, unencumbered with wife or family.

What is sad about having to read as an occupation is that I now so rarely read for pleasure, as once I would do during my days on the land or in the British Council. After trudging for much of a day through the lowlands of contemporary fiction, I am too tired for the mountains in the evening and sit back and listen to music instead. In retirement I should like to return again to George Moore, to Milton, to Smollett, to Wordsworth, to Balzac—Clifford Kitchin, the novelist, once told me that the greatest benefit that he had derived from his large private income was that he had had the time to read every word that Balzac had ever written. But when (unless he is a Clifford Kitchin or an Agatha Christie) can a professional writer ever decide to retire? Most of us—the sales of novels dwindling, P.L.R. still on the horizon—must, like a Greek peasant's donkey, go on and on till we drop. But, on reflection, I think that I really prefer it to be like that. I am seldom totally happy except when I am totally absorbed in writing.

ARTHUR KOESTLER

'Reading is bad for your eyes.' My father's voice still dimly echoes through the vaults of memory. I was an only child, born in the eighth year of my parents' marriage, over-protected, cosseted and bullied. Exerting my (perfectly healthy) eyes in school was unavoidable; but reading at home, and particularly by artificial light, had to be avoided for my own good. After a long battle—weeks? months? there are no clocks in the vaults—marked by tantrums, reprisals and wheedlings, a compromise was reached: before going to bed, I was permitted to read ten printed pages—'and not a line more, once and for all'. Although cheating should have been easy, the moral imperative was so strong for an undefinable period of time that I did not dare to exceed the allotted ration. But I do remember distinctly that the first book I read on this instalment plan was a Hungarian children's story about *A Tányértalpu Tekintetes Ur**—'The Adventures of the Honourable Flatfooted Teddybear Esquire'. The story was all the more thrilling because the kindly Esquire had a foolish little nephew, whom he always had to rescue from the most hair-

*My mother was Viennese, my father Hungarian, and I was brought up bilingually.

raising situations. To stop at the end of the statutory ten pages was as tantalizing as the abrupt ending of a cliff-hanger episode in the days of the silent film serials.

Though I am unable to tell how long the ten-page-a-day régime lasted, it had a lasting effect on my reading habits. To read fiction for pleasure (as distinct from schoolbooks which convey Knowledge) not only meant nibbling at the forbidden fruit, but nibbling slowly, to make the ration last longer and get the full flavour of every bite. I like to speculate what the effect would have been if my parents had rationed *time* instead of space, allowing, say, ten minutes reading instead of ten pages. Then, obviously, I would have devoured the printed signs as fast as I could, to cram as much as possible into the allotted time-span—devouring rather than savouring. As it happened, I have remained an exceedingly slow reader of fiction, unable to skip, intent on getting all my money's worth out of an imaginary ration. 'Schoolbooks', on the other hand, whether works of science, history or politics, have remained in a different category, demanding an altogether different reading technique—sniffing, browsing, skipping details, extracting the essence. Fiction-reading is still space-rationed, learning constrained only by the limits of time.

Being an only child, and (owing to another quirk of my parents) deprived of play-mates, had its compensations: once the rationing system collapsed, I became a full-time reader with little else to occupy or distract me. After Flatfoot and other children's books—the Grimms, Andersen, and ghastly Struwwelpeter—the first outstanding landmark is Alice—in a Hungarian translation first, then in German, much later in the original. It is amazing how a masterpiece can survive the depradations inflicted by hack-translators, and even in mutilated versions evoke world-wide resonances. But then, children are a cosmopolitan lot, with remarkably uniform tastes, shared mythologies and archetypal heroes; differentiation of culture-patterns and individual preferences come only later on. Thus the small Austro-Hungarian bookworm's diet in the Edwardian age consisted of a kind of Pan-European pot-pourri of Robinson Crusoe, Gulliver, Don Quixote, Till Eulenspiegel; of Karl May, Jules Verne, Fenimore Cooper—much the same menu as that of an English prep-school boy. What Chomsky calls 'the deep structures' underlying all languages appear to have their equivalent in the evolution of literary taste.

Its differentiation seems to set in around puberty. But it proceeds stepwise. During the early stages, the responses of the primordial taste-buds are modified by acquired tastes, and these are largely dependent on prevailing literary fashions. Truly individual taste—I knows what I likes *and* I knows why I likes it—develops only later on—if ever. I suspect that during most of my adolescence I was stuck in the first stage. At that period, Scandinavian writers were the rage in Austria—not only Strindberg and Ibsen, but Selma Lagerlöf, Pontoppidan, Aage Madelung, Jacobsen and Knut Hamsun. I read them all; the only one who made an impression was Hamsun, but it was deep and lasting. He made me discover the art of leaving out—an art which the early Hemingway brought to perfection and the late Hemingway reduced to caricature. (I had always thought that Hamsun had been a major influence on Hemingway—and before his death he confirmed this piece of deduction to our joint Norwegian publisher, Harald Grieg.)

Thus if I am to single out the first major impact, it was Hamsun—and it initiated at the same time the first steps towards individual discrimination. It all too quickly led to strong idiosyncrasies—violent hatreds of, or infatuations with, an author or a particular work. Thus I worshipped Dostoyevsky (*Crime and Punishment, The Possessed*) and detested Henry James (all of it); loved Oscar Wilde ('We are all in the gutter, but some of us are looking at the stars') and was repelled by G. B. Shaw; admired Stendhal and turned a cold eye on Flaubert. Literary appreciation should embrace the whole spectrum of the rainbow, but inevitably it becomes polarized like a magnetic field. At least that is my experience.

After the Scandinavians came a Russian period, interrupting for a while the steady flow of German, English and French literature at school and at home. It is quite surprising, in retrospect, through what a mass of bulky tomes even a slow worm can eat its way, if deprived of other fun and games. There was also a brief love-affair with Hungarian poetry—after we had moved from Budapest to Vienna and I felt homesick. (But what's the point dropping names like Vörösmarty, Endre Ady or Attila Jozsef in front of English readers when Hungarian, owing to its long, onomatopoetic words, rich in dark vowels, is one of the most untranslatable of languages? I once read to Auden in Ischia an English translation of mine of a poem by Attila Jozsef. He judged it passable, then asked me to read the Hungarian original, of which he understood not a word, only the music. When I had finished, he said: 'Throw the translation away.')

Among other favourite poets were Rilke, Goethe, Heine, Hölderlin and Byron, roughly in that order; the French symbolists; small slices out of T. S. Eliot, Christopher Fry and Dylan Thomas came much later. But the Bard loomed large on the horizon of my secondary school in Baden bei Wien, where we were taught that there are seven German Classics in the Pantheon: Klopstock, Wieland, Lessing, Herder, Goethe, Schiller and Shakespeare. The last named had been annexed and naturalized on the strength of the outstanding translations of Schlegel, Tieck and Baudissin, which can claim the status of classics in their own right, and of which we learned large chunks by heart. When I saw my first *Hamlet* at the Old Vic, the German text sounded in my ears like a whispered running commentary (*Sein oder nichtsein ist hier die Frage* ...). And when in the interval, John Strachey, who was my host, asked me how I liked it, I answered in all sincerity that the translation was marvellous.

*

Literature, then, was all very well as a guilty passion; but the principal heroes of my youth were Darwin and Spencer, Kepler, Newton and Mach; Edison, Herz and Marconi—the Buffalo Bills of the frontiers of science. And my Bible was Ernst Haeckel's *Die Weltraetsel.* In this popular classic of the turn of the century, seven 'Riddles of the Universe' were listed; of these, six appeared 'definitely solved' (including the Origin of Life), while the seventh—Freedom of the Will—was declared not to be a riddle at all but an unscientific illusion.

'Man as a social and moral being was without interest, a speck in the universe, and his history a dance of dust stirred up by the vacuum cleaner. The fascinating thing about man, and his only aspect worth studying, was the chemistry of his tissues, the algebra of his heredity, his descent from the monkeys, and the switchboard mechanism of his brain.'*

Which goes to show that, though born in 1905, I had been a true child of the nineteenth century—the century of crude philosophies and arrogant over-simplifications, which lingered on into the twentieth, until the First World War brought it to an end with a bang.

From here onward my private Pantheon becomes overcrowded. *La recherche de la paternité* is a favourite pastime of literary critics—genealogical quest for the 'formative influences', the ancestral genes which moulded a writer's style or his philosophical outlook. I have just been guilty of indulging in the game by referring to Hamsun's influence on Hemingway. But it is no more than a game, because such influences do not work along the simple straight lines of a genealogical table but rather like the threads woven into a Persian carpet, absorbed by the pattern of the whole, interacting with other threads, impossible to isolate from them. Besides, the pattern itself is subject to change; it may become frayed or discoloured in patches, or may even be re-woven in its entirety out of the same threads. Thus I am able to follow, up to a point, some of the threads or leitmotifs which dominated my particular design

* *Arrow in the Blue.*

at twenty, thirty, and so on; but torn out of their context they mean little. There is a violent red thread which leads from Marx, Engels and Lassale to Lenin and Trotsky, then breaks and vanishes into the noon-tide darkness. (Was the journey really necessary? The outcome was already predicted in Büchner's *Death of Danton.*) There is another thread which leads from Levy Brühl (*Primitive Mentality, How Natives Think*) to Freud and Jung. (Levy Brühl, now either forgotten or dismissed as an 'armchair anthropologist', had a powerful impact on both through his emphasis on the irrational, magic substratum in the mind of supposedly Rational Man.) There is a sort of ultra-violet thread which starts with Einstein and Niels Bohr, the founders of relativity and quantum physics, then wends its labyrinthine course to Heisenberg, Schrödinger and Pauli into the cloud of unknowing where space, time and matter no longer mean what they meant, causality and determinism are dethroned, and the future becomes unpredictable. There is a coarse thread leading from Pavlov's conditioned reflexes through Watson to Skinner's behaviourism and ending tied up in an ugly knot *Beyond Freedom and Dignity.* A similar dead end threatened the evolution of the theory of evolution, if one compared the exhilarating messages of Lamarck and Darwin with either the dusty answers of Monod's *Chance and Necessity* or the auto-hypnotic optimism in Teilhard's view of the *Phenomenon of Man.* And so on. As I have tried to sum it up elsewhere:

> In my youth I regarded the universe as an open book, printed in the language of physical equations and social determinants, whereas now it appears to me as a text written in invisible ink of which, in our rare moments of grace, we are able to decipher a small fragment ...

OLIVIA MANNING

Books I Have Read

My journey out of literary darkness reads like one of those post-Wellsian novels much written in the '30s: lower middle-class hero, unlettered but aspirant, comes upon a copy of *John o'London's Weekly* and never looks back. A whole new area of life is revealed to him—an area where books are Important. Heroines tended to belong to an upper class and revolted not against ignorance but bourgeois values. The two would meet in the middle middle where intellectuals end up, imagining they have achieved a state of classlessness.

Before the revelation came to me, I floundered about on my own, passing from fairy stories to school stories and arriving with a shock of revelation at my first 'grown up' book: a novel by Rider Haggard.

In childhood I was given *The Water Babies, Alice,* Hans Andersen and *Red, Blue* and *Green Fairy Books,* all intended to keep me quiet. They did more than that. They inspired me to write my own fairy stories or, more probably, my own version of the stories I had read. My father, who had access to the stationery store on Whale Island, gave me large account books with marbled edges and rough black covers, which I filled with scribble, scribble, scribble like Mr Gibbon. When I tired of writing, I got down to the illustrations. For many years it was in the balance whether I was to be writer or artist. The question was settled in the usual way. I could afford pen and paper but not much else.

From those days I have a vivid memory of a children's book that had a story about fireworks; the fireworks took on a life of their own and with a rush and a scream, burst out of their packets calling 'Come on, boys' and were off in search of adventure. The thing that impressed me about this book was the mysterious way in which it disappeared. I had found it in a linen cupboard, hidden no doubt by my father whose discredited friends would give him gifts for me which he dared not pass on. I never knew what happened to it.

My father, who had made his own discoveries during his watches on board ship, owned a Shakespeare, a Longfellow (whom he often quoted), a Tennyson and a Hood. They were old books with two-column pages of tiny type and I imagined they were deadly dull. Together with the *Bab Ballads*, which amused me immensely, and the *Ingoldsby Legends*, they comprised the family library. There were also a few novels. Once when I was mooning about, needing diversion, my father offered me an early edition of *Adam Bede*. My mother took it from me, saying it was not a 'nice' book, and as the pages were closely printed and the illustrations grim, I accepted her opinion. Many years passed before I discovered how wrong she had been.

I used to hang around the public library, sensing that somewhere there if one could find it, was the answer to the mystifying boredom of existence. The library at North End, Portsmouth—I think it is still there—was a narrow red building with the name 'Carnegie' embossed on a scroll of yellow cement. Inside it was nothing like the libraries today. It had become a municipal library but it was still dedicated to the Carnegie principle of educating the working classes. The borrower was allowed to take only one novel and with it must take a general book of an improving nature. Finding books was an arduous task. A slotted metal curtain hung beside the librarians' counter and into the slots were slipped the book numbers, black for those that were 'in', red for those that were 'out'. The borrower must first consult one of the catalogues that, grimy with fingering, contained the numbers of the hidden and guarded books. Having found a number, he had then to ask for a form and fill in not only the particulars of the book but of himself: name, address, date of birth, position of the sun at time of making a request, &c., &c. This done, he stood in a queue to enter his form. More often than not, while all this was going on, the number would change from black to red and the search must begin again. There were many more borrowers than there were desirable books. The rivalry was terrible. Small children were at the mercy of larger children who would push them out of the queue.

When I first went through the catalogues, I was not tall enough to read the upper parts of the pages so I was limited to what I could find below. Being still at the fairy tale stage, I pursued for weeks a book with the promising title of *The Princess Orchid.* When I at last found it in, I sadly discovered there had been an error in the catalogue. The title was, in fact, *The Priceless Orchid* and the book was a sober account of a search for new orchid varieties.

Hans Andersen was the favourite of those days. I still think that Finmark is an enormous ice palace where Kay tries with ice splinters to spell 'Eternity' by the gleam of the Northern Lights. I so identified myself with the Ugly Duckling that, much later in life, I believed I had only to reach Bloomsbury and beautiful swans—they might be Virginia Woolf and Vanessa Bell—would come sailing to welcome me and caress me with their beaks. I did in the end reach Bloomsbury, only to find that whatever else Hans Andersen knew, he did not know much about the habits of swans.

'Will you introduce me to Virginia Woolf?' I begged my first publisher, who was on the fringe of her group. He stared in astonishment at my presumption. 'Certainly not,' he said, 'she hates young women writers. She would cut you to pieces.'

I was unpleasantly fascinated by Grimms' stories that were not meant for children, being German folk tales collected by the Brothers Grimm. 'Look what I'm reading,' I said, showing my neighbour in class a story called *The Glass Coffin.* She turned distastefully away with the crushing statement: 'My mother does not permit me to read stories like that.'

My own reading was unsupervised. My parents had other things to think about. I grew out of fairy stories when the situation at home was at its worst. My mother made it plain to us that only for our sake did she remain in the same house with our erring father. My brother and I felt guilty that because of us our parents lived in a state of alternating uproar and sullen sulks. I retreated into *Little Folks* and *Chatterbox*, where the children were all several cuts above our social status. I told other girls that I had a nurse and a nursery and would soon be going to boarding-school. Of course no one believed me and I gained a reputation as a liar and show-off. For Christmas and birthdays I wanted books by Angela Brazil and I collected stout volumes printed on woolly paper with titles like *The Luckiest Girl in the School* or *The Prettiest* or *The Most Popular*—none of which enviable estates was mine.

The school story phase ended overnight when I borrowed, probably by accident, my first 'grown-up' novel. It was one of Rider Haggard's Zulu stories and, being the last of a trilogy, was called *Finished.* I read the three volumes backwards. The excitement of entering the adult book world was so great that I ran a temperature and was suspected of having caught a chill. For a memorable period, between the ages of twelve and fourteen, I read through Rider Haggard. The library, as usual, could not supply my needs and I spent all my pocket money on small greenish-grey books with coarse buff pages: the Rider Haggard cheap edition. Each cost two shillings, so I could buy one a fortnight. I became an authority on Zulu history, but they were not all African novels. I remember a love story called *Star of the Sea* in which the lovers, pure and noble (the woman, I think, was married to someone else), walked at twilight along a shore that was littered with bones and coffin scraps washed out from a seaside cemetery by the encroaching sea. The scene seemed to me the quintessence of the romantic macabre but when I looked at it again some years later, I found it unreadable.

I was now being plagued by the question: how did I intend to earn my living? It was all very well wanting to be a painter or a writer or something of that sort, but one must first have the means to keep oneself. I was advised to find a secure job and write or paint in my spare time. After some months of argument, I was put to learn shorthand and typewriting. I learnt to type with all fingers, a useful accomplishment for a writer, but I was no good at shorthand. I could write it down but I could not read it back. I never had a secure job. I lost job after job because I could take none of them seriously. My future, I felt, was elsewhere.

At the commercial college, a teacher—the same one that lent me *John o'London's Weekly*—asked me if I had read Shaw's plays. *Read* them? Did one read plays? There was little chance of seeing them as the pit at the Theatre Royal cost 3/6d and the gallery crowd was reputed to be so rough and wild, it was not safe to go there. I found *Plays Pleasant and Unpleasant* and flung myself into Shaw as into a rough sea where swimmers cavorted and shrieked with laughter amid the buffetings of the waves. I was delighted, and needed more and more of him. I saved up to buy him and still have some first editions acquired in those days. Shaw's challenge to the bourgeois conventions, prejudices and snobberies in which I had grown up roused me to a state of exultation. I told myself he had put paid to God—meaning to the petty social tyrants of provincial life who would, I felt, if they could, hold me down as a thumb holds down a cork in water.

By now I had finished with the little North End library and was finding my way through the Central Library that adjoined the Municipal College where I took evening classes in painting.

The antiquated borrowing system had been scrapped: the shelves were open to borrowers but the library itself still had a Dickensian air of disorder. The shelves, all of different heights and depths, wandered about in all directions. Many of the books, bound in cast-iron covers, had been there for half a century. Behind the library there was a park that was peculiar among Portsmouth parks because it had cages with a few undistinguished mammals and a family of peacocks. It was to the melancholy cries of these birds that I discovered the 'moderns' of my youth: D. H. Lawrence (I wept all the way to school when he died), Aldous Huxley, William Gerhardi, Virginia Woolf, Wyndham Lewis, Katherine Mansfield, Norman Douglas—exhilarating writers who kept me writing myself, away in my small bedrooms where, sitting between the door and the window, I caught a never-ending string of colds in the head.

I came upon Jung's *Psychology of the Unconscious* and brought it home to devour it. My father picked the book up after a row with my mother and sat brooding over it. I was embarrassed, feeling it was not a suitable book for him to read and I hoped he was too distraught to understand it. Later, in his gentle way, he came to me and quietly told me he did not think it was a suitable book for me to read.

My mother's only concern was for the harm I might do myself in the marriage market. When she saw me with the *Times Literary Supplement*, she clicked her tongue in disapproval and said, 'Young men do not like girls who reads papers like that.' A lot I cared. I was going to a city where there were young men with more advanced ideas.

My imagination was particularly heightened by the enthusiasms of Middleton Murry. He wrote at a tumultuous pace about Russian writers, especially about Dostoyevsky, whom I determined to read for myself. When I eventually obtained a copy of *The Brothers Karamazov*, I realized that here was a writer as far above Shaw as Shaw was above Rider Haggard. I went from one library to another in search of Dostoyevsky's novels. I became quite drunk on the few that I found. I put in Request Cards and outlying libraries were searched on my behalf but, in those days, library buying was as haphazard as my reading and no one thought to buy the complete output of a writer. I went in search of Chekhov, Turgenev, Gogol, anyone with a Russian name, and, avid to renew the flavour of one writer, I was usually forced to adjust my literary palate to a different one. There was as much frustration as excitement for me during those adolescent days of wine and roses.

When I reached London, a friend, who was a student of French writing, insisted that I must read Flaubert and Proust. I dutifully did so but they did not transport me as the Russians did. My first published novel was read for Cape by William Plomer, who asked me about my aims and aspirations. 'I want to write like Dostoyevsky,' I told him. He smiled kindly on me and said he thought I would do well enough if I just wrote like myself.

My friend, continuing to further my education, introduced me to the works of James Joyce and gave me a copy of *Ulysses* bought in Paris. It was a slim volume on India paper, hand-bound in white, and it went with me to Rumania, Greece, the Middle East and home again. Then, during the hungry post-war years, someone stole it from my bookcase. The giver had written round the title 'From Ulysses, the Wanderer and Deceiver'. If anyone ever comes upon it, I would dearly like to have it back.

I am not sure why I read so few of the classical English novelists. I think I associated them with school and the way in which school reading made everything seem dull. My husband, when we married just before the war, was shocked to find I hardly knew Jane Austen or the Brontës, and had never read Henry James. After the war I bought, rather expensively, a row of Henry James first editions that were mostly worn ex-library copies, only to find that I could have bought several of them direct from the publisher as these first editions were still in print. 'Why,' Henry James sadly asked a friend, 'does everyone buy Marie Corelli and Hall Caine, and nobody buy me?' Alas, poor Henry James, he should have known the answer. Was it not an American who said that no one has ever lost money by underestimating the taste of the general public?

At last, quite late in life, I came to Trollope and Dickens and Thackeray. Passing through a period of great anxiety, unable to sleep, I started reading *Our Mutual Friend*. The first pages seemed to me unpleasantly melodramatic. 'Impossible,' I told myself: 'I knew I could never read Dickens'—then, suddenly, the magic took hold of me and I became a Dickens addict. I did not need to search through the libraries. We had a complete Dickens on the shelf and I read one novel after another, entranced, knowing myself fortunate that I had found him in time of need. When I reached the end, my grief was that there was not more. I went on to Trollope, whom I had to borrow, and was back in the old condition of 'Who's in? Who's out?' unable to find half the Trollope I wanted. Now I am still in the midst of Thackeray.

I amuse my properly educated friends by bursting out: 'What a wonderful character, Mr Dorritt!' 'How brilliant Trollope at his best!' 'What fun Thackeray can be!' Surely all that is taken for granted! I have to explain that I am not re-reading these great novelists. I am reading them for the first time.

And what am I going to do when I come to the end of Thackeray? Having created a habit of night reading, my life is a search for longer and longer books. I do not want them to end. I do not want to leave the author in hand. I could scarcely bear to change from Thomas Mann to Hermann Hesse. It was painful to leave Hesse and face up to John Cowper Powys. Worse still to leave Powys and pass on to &c., &c.

I wish my writing friends would write longer novels. But the modern novel, which tends to be subtle rather than profound, entertaining rather than instructive, unmoral and reflective of our chaos, is too disturbing a companion for the long, despondent hours of night. I read them by daylight. The only contemporaries who seem to me to offer a fabric in which I can lose myself are Patrick White and Saul Bellow. And they are still living. One can ask for more of them in reasonable hope of getting it.

IRIS MURDOCH

I read stories, also poetry, also philosophy, theology, politics. The first book I was aware of was *Treasure Island* and I re-read it at intervals. Basic diet: nineteenth-century English and Russian novels, plus Henry James, plus Proust. I like adventure stories and romances of almost any kind (not detective stories except for Raymond Chandler): anything from *Sir Gawain* and *Morte d'Arthur* and *The Tale of Genji* to *The Lord of the Rings*, P. G. Wodehouse and *Tintin*. The higher loves: Homer and Shakespeare. I need and re-visit very various poems and poets, some Greeks and Romans, English seventeenth century, all sorts of religious and love poetry, Yeats, Eliot, Auden, haiku. The philosophers I have fed most upon are Plato, Kant, Kierkegaard, Nietzsche, Wittgenstein and Simone Weil. I love a clear thinker and a plain speaker: Hume, Wittgenstein, Freud. Home: the *Iliad*, certain plays of Shakespeare. Fun: any good yarn.

HAROLD PINTER

In my teens I read Dylan Thomas, Rimbaud, Hemingway, Henry Miller, Keats, Dos Passos, Céline, Cardus, D. H. Lawrence, Huxley, Gerard Manley Hopkins, Virginia Woolf, Pound, Laforgue, Euripides, Villon, Webster, Tourneur, Eliot, Joyce, Yeats and Shakespeare.

In my twenties I read, apart from the above, Kafka, Beckett, Emily Brontë, Auden, Wilfred Owen, Blake, Coleridge, De Sade, Matthew Arnold, Tolstoy, Sartre, Camus, Donne, Dostoyevsky.

In my thirties and forties I read, apart from the above, Hardy, Pope, Solzhenitsyn, Larkin, Proust.

I read a great deal of poetry.

PETER PORTER

Neither my mother nor my father was a reader of books. I grew up in suburban Brisbane during the Depression, when there was very little money about, so that, while I was nominally a middle-class child, in practice we were very poor. I have few recollections of reading when young, though I suppose I learned to do so quickly, as I could read by the time I went to school, aged four and a half. The first book I can recall clearly was a selection from world literature which I must have seen in an aunt's house. In it I came across *The Ancient Mariner* with illustrations (not Doré's), and this was the first time I had noticed poetry. I suppose I must have read *Winnie the Pooh* and the like, but I think that was later. I looked occasionally at the Bible, though my parents were not believers. I'd got into the habit of going to Sunday school—for the company, I imagine. *The Book of Common Prayer* impressed me more than the Bible, less for the glories of Cranmer's prose than for the fact that it was intoned in church and so easier to remember. My father had been raised a Baptist and my mother a Presbyterian: what should be more natural than that their only child, almost absurdly over-protected, should join the Church of England, the first sign of aspirations to a higher social order.

The event which changed my life was my mother's death in 1938 when I was nine. My guardian was a lady whose husband had made money. She was a great believer in the public-school system (Australian variety and ludicrously out of date by English standards) and she pushed my father into sending me to boarding school. I stayed at three different schools for nine years, and it was there that my reading habits were formed. My education was very bad—it was wartime and the best masters were in the army—but it introduced me to serious literature. It's quite possible that had I not been forced to study poetry (Shakespeare and the Victorians chiefly) I should never have concerned myself with it at all. But my reading in my teens was quite haphazard, ranging from highbrow histories to the worst sort of adventure books and popular novels like *Anthony Adverse* and *The Sun is My Undoing*. I read hundreds of trashy books and few good ones—all of Bulldog Drummond, Biggles and the rest. The only poet I knew well was Browning, and he has remained a favourite to this day. I had never heard of any modern poet, not even T. S. Eliot, until a year after I left school and went to work on the local newspaper. By this time I was already writing poetry in great quantities, having started in my last year at school. I then met other poets, much better informed than myself, and in a matter of five years before sailing for England gave myself a crash course in modern poetry. Such a history reveals immediately that I am largely self-taught and therefore very ill-read. But some books have had a potent effect on me and I list them below, with a few comments in some cases.

Tolstoy: *What is Art? and other essays*. I read this at school long before I attempted any of the novels. I still think it is a vastly entertaining book, with a fair claim to being the most eccentric collection of opinions ever published. Tolstoy on Beethoven and Shakespeare is almost unbelievable, but he is a tonic to anyone sated on academic orthodoxy. I find his criticism more interesting than his novels.

Thucydides: *The Peloponnesian War*. The best work of history

I've read. It has a marvellous sense of approaching doom. I read it, of course, in English.

Fifteen Poets. A school text published in the 'thirties with selections from fifteen major English poets. The selections were made by contemporary English poets and the book was published by O.U.P. W. H. Auden introduced Byron; Louis MacNeice, Coleridge; Edmund Blunden, Shelley. I got my first taste of Auden's originality in his essay, without knowing who he was. All I knew was that I loved Byron and was entirely convinced by the man who presented him in this book.

I now come to my immediate post-school reading.

W. H. Auden: *The Age of Anxiety* and *Letters from Iceland.* I read Auden from the middle of his career backwards. I bought *The Age of Anxiety* when it came out and I can say, in the approved corny way, that it made me decide to be a poet. I didn't understand it, and I was overwhelmed by the language. I saw at once (and I have never wanted to revise the opinion) that poetry is not a matter of having something to say but rather of having a style to say something in. I went on from Auden circa 1948 to the 'thirties poetry, the plays, and the long poems. *Letters from Iceland* I found and still do one of the most charming books I have read. My envy of Auden and MacNeice in their tight world of clever people who knew each otherwas colossal. I'm sure it induced me to come to England.

Mozart's Letters, edited by Emily Anderson. Mozart's genius impressed me from the start as the greatest miracle in the world, and I found his letters the most human, moving, even tragic documents I'd yet read. How marvellous it would be to have a similar collection written by Shakespeare.

The Paintings of Hieronymus Bosch. I forget which edition this was, and I certainly didn't read the text with much attention, but the pictures fascinated me. Bosch was the first painter I really liked. Only recently have I developed any eye for pictures and now my taste favours Florentines like Castagno and Piero di Cosimo, but no one has struck me as Bosch did when I was young.

Byron: *Don Juan. Pace* Pope, the only readable long poem in English. Still the best book for a long sea voyage. If Ariosto and Dante were in English, they might be readable too.

Christopher Smart: *Jubilate Agno.* I first read this Bedlam poem in 1951 and it has influenced me more than any other single work. I know it isn't a good policy to esteem authors for their unreasonableness, but I find Smart's strange litany a definition of what I think poetry is. I read bits of it almost every month.

Norman Cohn: *The Pursuit of the Millennium.* What a modern book of history should be. Cohn's account of the eschatological revolutionaries of Europe in the Dark and Middle Ages is the most important work of research I know. It makes the study of history as a matter of sovereign states seem outmoded.

Thomas Mann: *The Magic Mountain* and *Doctor Faustus.* These may not be the world's greatest novels, but to me they feel as though they are. It took me a long time to read *The Magic Mountain*, but the slow progress was due to admiration. I wish I knew enough German to read them as Mann left them.

Wallace Stevens: *Collected Poems.* The great modern clarifier and true exorcizer of the wicked spirit of Yeats.

This list doesn't include the poems of Donne, Rochester, Pope and Clare, Shakespeare's, Wycherley's and Farquhar's plays or most of the great English novels. The books above are the singletons in my experience. There is, after all, no limit to the quantity of good writing in the world.

FREDERIC RAPHAEL

My father was always telling me that reading was an essential part of my education, but that cannot have been the only reason why I was for so long unwilling to open a book. True, I thought it enough that I should jump through the required scholastic hoops, which I did with regularly rewarded agility, without burdening myself with voluntary fatigues, but it was equally true that I had no clear idea of what either my father or my masters meant by serious reading. It was not customary, even in the sixth form at my public school, for anyone to go so far as to recommend a specific extra-curricular work. We had one period of English a week. It was taken by a sports master who was too thic to teach anything else, apart from getting it out to the wings and not dribbling in the penalty area. He was the first adult ever to say to me, 'I'm not as clever as you,' and the amazement I felt remains evidence of the effectiveness of the indoctrination I received.

Of course I read the Classics. It was, as they said at Charterhouse, where scholars were known as 'hash [work[pros', what I was paid to do. But the traditional Classics were carefully docked of all passionate or political reference. Even today

Fordyce's fig-leaved edition of deathless Catullus (Oxford, 1961) omits the indecorous poems. Until I stumbled, very late, on Jane Harrison's *Prolegomena To The Study Of Greek Religion* (surely one of the most thrilling, if now out-dated, works of scholarship ever written) and then on Professor George Thomson's *Aeschylus and Athens,* I had little notion of the bloody origins of the Olympians or of the structure of ancient, or any other, societies. Strangely, it was Charterhouse which produced both Robert Graves and Peter Green, whose assaults on established ideas have had such an abrasive effect on Classical studies. *I, Claudius* and *Claudius the God* were the first books that turned marble into flesh for me. (*King Jesus* performed an equally humanizing service in another respect.) Green lacks Graves's literary gifts, but his *Essays In Antiquity* and other volumes, down to *The Shadow Of The Parthenon,* are not only full of sparks but light new fires. Who can read them without hurrying to the library with a list?

In my lonely adolescence I sought truth more than beauty. I had no sense of belonging to a society. I was a so-called Jew parked among so-called Christians; I was born in America and had my home in England; I had no brothers or sisters and I claimed no friends. Like the young Sartre, I became an expert in dissimulation. I hummed along with the hymns (though I did not bow my head in the Creed) and concealed my dissidence like the Spartan boy with his fox. One day—I must have been sixteen—my mother caught mumps. I could neither go in to see her, lest I catch it, nor leave the flat, lest I seem indifferent. I was bored enough to take a book from the grown-up shelves. What curious instinct led me to *Of Human Bondage*? I read it in one day. In one day, so I was ready to believe, it taught me about Life. It also determined me to become a novelist. Was I not as unhappy as Philip Carey? My wretchedness and my sense of destiny combined, curse and benediction, to confirm me in my purpose. When I read of Philip's schooldays, they seemed almost identical with mine (save that Philip suffered from a club-foot and I from being a

Jew), and when I read of his sexual adventures, I could not but hope that I might share those too. Miss Wilkinson, Philip's appalling initiator, did not appal me. In the secret heat of my frustrations, I could have wished for so direct a lady. (On wet afternoons in the Charing Cross Road, I stood, painfully ithyphallic, turning the pages of Van der Velde's *Ideal Marriage* at the counter of bookshops—one chapter per shop, to foil Foyle's disapproval—seeking proof that I was neither freak nor lunatic.) What other children were lucky enough to learn in the gutter I had to find in books.

Before Maugham, it had been William and the Saint and Biggles, the common pantheon of common children of the 'forties, though my favourite book was *Sixty Famous Trials,* Socrates to the Crumbles Murder. ('What have you got there?' 'The body in three pieces,' was the terse reply.) It gave me a lifelong fantasy of myself as Sir Edward Marshall Hall and a nightmare dread of Mr Justice 'Acid-drop' Avory. After *Of Human Bondage*, I believed myself 'wryly detached', in the style of the Master. The epigram seemed to me a magic form; it enabled one to be both sardonic and successful, for it was applauded by the very people at whom its barbs were aimed. I read Coward and Laurence Housman and noted with what very short measure a playwright might make a name.

Between school and Cambridge came sexual and literary emancipation. I left my Zarathustra on the Northern Line, but I was transported by Nietzsche's lofty venom, and remain so. In those months I read *Sons and Lovers; Le Rouge et le Noir; Point Counter Point; The Trial; Crime and Punishment; Smoke* and *Anna Karenina* and *Madame Bovary* (oh, and all the Raymond Chandler I could find). Blessed Penguin, blessed Everyman! I was now so compulsive a reader that I ceased to look up at the world at all. I walked from bus to bus, jinking intuitively like a wing three-quarter, my head always down.

I was not interested only in great literature. The brother-in-law of the girl I loved (and love) was a Communist and I was amazed at his insolence (McCarthy was rising fast): he did not bother to hide it! He lent me many books—*The Iron Heel* and *The Road To Wigan Pier* made the deepest impression—and I was condescendingly grateful that a man who had been a Bevin boy could instruct a Cambridge scholar. (I had not been as politically null as all that: *Guilty Men* had affected me enough for me to be the only Labour supporter in my nice prep school during the 1945 election.)

I was eager to lose my illusions. During my first year at Cambridge I was tipped off to read *Language, Truth and Logic.* The God of Charterhouse Chapel, that unbending Headmaster of the Universe, and Jesus Christ, his only begotten Head Monitor, stumbled and fell dead at my feet: non-sense personified and definitively unverifiable. The world had only to be cleaned of metaphysics, the place of Reason established and patient social engineering would clean up the few remaining problems. Had not Popper's *The Open Society and Its Enemies* cut down Plato and Hegel and Marx, the three great unreadables, with one mighty blast of chain-shot? Wittgenstein, at that time the password to a sense of mystic brotherhood, not yet a mere *amuse-gueule* for the higher name-dropper, mopped up the metaphysical survivors and took them off for therapeutic re-thinking. (The soul had been taken care of by Ryle's psychotomizing *Concept of Mind.*) Arthur Koestler's contribution to *The God That Failed*, along with *Spanish Testament* and *Darkness at Noon*, lent authority to my disdain for the institutional left. Siegfried Giedion's *Space, Time and Architecture* persuaded me that Architecture, selfless, three-dimensional morality, might provide the new Guardians, ethical aesthetes one and all. 'We' were through with systems, at last. (*Why You Lose at Bridge*, by S. J. Simon, was another congenial blow at system-building, the Vienna bidding system, and declared that functional pragmatism would beat formal rigidity every time. Mrs Guggenheim and Mr Smug still shuffle, bid and play in my fantasy world, though I no longer circulate the pasteboards, as my old friend Guy Ramsey would say.) I like to see the Gods unmasked and continue to read debunkers with scarcely mitigated credulity. How many lies we were told, we war-time schoolboys! Above all, I became obsessed with what is now called 'the Holocaust'. The selfish pain I had felt at school turned to rage as much at the indifference of the British and the Americans as at the brutality of the Germans, a rage unsatisfied to this day. Its fuel through the years has been steadily supplied: Primo Levi's *If This Is A Man*; *The Terzien Requiem; While Six Million Died; The Final Solution;* Norman Cohn's *Warrant for Genocide*; Hilberg's *Destruction of the European Jews*; Sartre's *The Anti-Semite* and Malcolm Hay's *Europe and the Jews*, even Malaparte's *Kaput*, with all its ambivalence. However comfortable my circumstances, however 'accepted' I seem to be, I am privileged never to be able to forget what I was lucky enough never to experience. All Utopian 'solutions', however amiable, arouse my unquenched scepticism.

Almost alone of my contemporaries, I sometimes think, I did not read English at Cambridge. I could read, therefore, with an irresponsible and uninformed greed. Primed by Edmund Wilson's *Classics and Commercials,* I discovered America through American writing: Upton Sinclair's *The Jungle* gave a meaty impression of the city of my birth; then came Faulkner (*Light in August, Intruder in the Dust* rather than the *Sartoris* cycle), the Hemingway of the short stories, Nathaniel West, and above all, Sinclair Lewis and John O'Hara. The trouble with great writers is that they intimidate the novice. Lewis and O'Hara impressed me with the vividness of their observation but they did not wear magisterial robes. Their style was accessible. Like Maugham they aimed to use simple words and keep the story moving. *Appointment in Samarra* taught me more about the writing of fiction than any other book. When my first novel came out, it was reviewed in the same batch as *Ten North Frederick*, and I was praised, in one of the weeklies, for my wit and lightness, which were flatteringly compared with O'Hara's ponderousness. It is the only good notice of which I have ever been ashamed. Maugham,

Lewis and O'Hara often let themselves down; all three were capable of very bad work, but they persuaded me that I could pad along behind them, and for that at least I remain grateful.

English poetry has never meant as much to me as I would have liked. I suspect that my lack of zeal is due largely to my loathing for T. S. Eliot. He and Yeats and Pound were the fastidious man's warrant for genocide and I continue to wonder how they, and many others in the tradition of the cultured, would have behaved had the heavy mob won the day and shod their metaphors with jackboots. (I am equally untouched by the Harold Nicolson-Bloomsbury axis, suspecting that for all their wonderful sensitivity—*The Waves* enraptured me at twenty—they too would have found reasons not to notice the cattle trucks en route from distasteful places to camps in gardenless regions of no abiding historical interest.) I still cling to a measure of realism as a specific against high-flown mythologies which contain human sacrifice as an incidental aspect of their 'imagery'. For my poets I look abroad: to Seferis (especially) and Cavafy, to Lorca and Neruda and Juan Ramon Jimenez. I try not to read only English, even though I am not a linguist. Balzac is a bore in translation; *Remembrance of Things Past* is not the same book as *A La Recherche Du Temps Perdu,* though I have yet to finish the latter. My joy in reading French and my love for France, which has survived both Algeria and realpolitikal Arabophilia, originated with *L'Express*, the old, hairy, unchic version, which led me to Sartre and to Mauriac, just as *A Narrow Street* had led me to the Rue de la Huchette. *Les Chemins de la Liberté* seemed to me the very essence of the grown-up novel, and I continue to have a furtive apprehension that only French literature is the real thing. The *Guide Michelin* remains my favourite spring book.

Boring old Henry James (enlivened by Edel's brilliant first biographical volumes) became a passion only quite recently, boring Dickens never. I prefer Thomas Mann to George Eliot and Svevo to Forster. *The Woman of Rome* led me to read all Moravia in the deceptively accessible Italian and he and Fellini and Antonioni have settled my vision of Italy. (*'Beh, le donne ...'*). I was finished with Cambridge before I happened on a book called *The Armed Vision* (an egghead paperback, bought in St Germain des Prés) and discovered the New Critics, then already rather old: Maud Bodkin, Blackmur, Empson, but above all Kenneth Burke. Burke's work has never been published in England. In my view, *The Philosophy of Literary Form* and *A Grammar of Motives,* for all their nimble pedantries, are vital reading for anyone concerned with the strategy of literature. (Burke's nimbleness enabled him to find a strategic justification for the Moscow Treason Trials, but I did not know that until I had become an admirer. His mind remains admirable, as, no doubt, does Mr Eliot's and the Pound of *The ABC of Reading* and, according to J. P. Sullivan, of *Homage to Sextus Propertius.*) The reading lists compounded from the inspiration of *The Armed Vision* still keep me busy. Sir Steven Runciman's *A History of the Crusades* served a similarly fruitful purpose: I went from the Kingdom of Jerusalem to Byzantium, so despised by my Romanophile schoolmasters, and loiter still.

I am reconciled to never catching up with the defects of my temper and education. I am a vulgar lover of books; possession no less than illumination excites me. When I reviewed fiction regularly, I was unable to match the world-weariness of my colleagues. A new book is a good book to me, until proved otherwise. Yet few contemporaries provoke my sense of urgency. Isaac Bashevis Singer and Nabokov, yes, but then are they contemporaries? How do they manage to be so remote and yet so immediate? Jerzy Kosinski and the late Gordon Meyer (especially his short stories and travel books like *The River and the People*—my autographed copy was lost in a Jamaican flood and I would pay well for another) have, as they say, got home to me; so did James Baldwin, until he began proving things. My friend Brian Glanville writes short stories with the readability of Maugham and from his *The Bankrupts* I learned that one might write about Jews without being accused of treating them too kindly. Oh, I admire many things by many people, but no one seems quite to say exactly what I want to hear, which is why, I suppose, I go on trying to say it myself.

ALAN SILLITOE

Mountains and Caverns

The first book I read, at the age of ten, was *Les Misérables*, by Victor Hugo. I'd heard it serialized as a play on the wireless, and when I saved enough money to get the book I was able to read such things as:

> Are the duties of the historians of hearts and souls inferior to those of the historians of external facts? Can we believe that Dante has less to say than Machiavelli? Is the lower part of civilization, because it is deeper and more gloomy, less important than the upper? Do we know the mountain thoroughly if we do not know the caverns?

On second thoughts perhaps I skipped that passage, rather than face the ignominy of not understanding it. More to my taste would have been: 'Ships and barricades are the only two battlefields from which escape is impossible.' And so is life itself. But I read the book again and again in the next ten years, till most of it was fixed firmly into me.

There was a public library less than a quarter of a mile from where we lived. The first time I went in I couldn't believe that so many books were free—at my disposal. I was astonished to see hundreds of clean and neatly stacked books, a catalogued treasure-house of handy volumes waiting to be borrowed three at a time. I had failed to win a scholarship to the grammar school, but what did it matter with so much knowledge free for all?

Classified as a child, I could only get at baby books, William books, works by Conan Doyle, Rider Haggard, John Buchan. I gluttonously read my way from Montezuma's Daughter to the flat on Baker Street (both equally remote), and then asked the librarian if I could move into the grown-ups' section.

But when he said yes, I went back to reading Victor Hugo, because *Les Misérables* and *The Man Who Laughed* and *The Hunchback of Notre Dame* and *The Toilers of the Sea* were closer to me than those aforementioned sub-classics of the English post-1870 Education Act literature. And rather than persist with Dickens, who for some reason I couldn't stand, I read books of travel (such as *France on Ten Pounds*) and books of instruction on how to write articles and stories, as well as histories, geography books, dictionaries—anything—apart from Hugo, with Dumas occasionally thrown in. A teacher at school, whose name was Charles Rowe, saw my interest in geography and politics and lent me G. D. H. Cole's *Social History of Post-war Europe*, a book beyond me at the time, though I appreciated his gesture.

I think *books* influenced me more than any title. I was entranced by the volume as an object, stiff covers between which were several hundred pages of magical symbols called print. I could flip them and cause a breeze against my cheek, thus demonstrating certain principles of physics. I could make a stack and see them from a few feet away as a pyramid of print, a Pennine of pages. They appeared to me as stepping-stones to some state that I didn't yet know about.

Books were plentiful. Books were cheap. In Frank Wore's second-hand shop downtown was a cellar with a vast table laden with books at threepence each, and once the war started and there was more money about I could afford at least one or two a week. In that cellar, where a coalfire burned on Saturday afternoons, and the smell of damp books and soot was so intense that I can still remember it clearly, no literary classic was beyond my reach. Yet I still preferred textbooks, crumbling lexicons, out of date one-volume encyclopaedias, old sixpenny cycling maps, Baedeker guidebooks—anything but fiction. I bought an immense leatherbound copy of the *Book of Job* in French, and read a few pages of that.

I hoarded books, and they caused a certain amount of resentment when I brought them into the house, especially from my father, who could not read or write, and who thought I should spend money on something more worthwhile, such as food or shoes.

But with books I could cut myself off from everybody in the house. I had a refuge—which my parents, brothers and sisters had not. If they wanted to escape they were stuck to the mains wireless. I had only to walk away with a book in my hand.

Books also took up space. They were intimidating. If you couldn't read, they were no good to you, so you wanted to kick them aside or sweep them off the table. When you did read, you went on reading, and the more you were absorbed, the quicker you got at the core of the book. The more you read, the more you wanted to read. Reading was mixed up with the cinema, *Comic Cuts,* and the *Radio Times.*

I once saw a pyramid of hundreds of dictionaries outside the school stokehole waiting to be burned. With a friend I climbed over the high wall during one summer holiday when the school was deserted but for the caretaker, and saw this heap of redundant books. We couldn't understand why they had not been given out free, for all of us to take home. Admitted, most were in bad condition, but there was much use in them yet. Along the wall, where they were waiting to be burned, it said in neatly painted white letters: CLEANLINESS IS NEXT TO GODLINESS—as if the world would be cleaner when fire had polished off these precious and attractive books of words. We descended from our perch and thieved as many good copies as we could carry away.

The Second World War came and went, and I still read only textbooks, and books about the war itself. It is almost true to say that I read nothing that was adult till I was twenty. My teens were passed on other matters. After work in the factory I studied navigation, mathematics and meteorology, as an air cadet. Then there was the usual adolescent courting and boozing thrown in, to pass any spare time that was left.

In Malaya—where I went as a wireless operator with the R.A.F.—I was stuck to a radio-set for fourteen hours at a stretch, and so had time to read. I'd brought in my kitbag from England a copy of *Les Misérables*, and the Old Testament. I met others who also read. A corporal threw me an abridged Penguin copy of *The Ragged-Trousered Philanthropists* after a long conversation about politics.

I picked up a volume which contained *Sevastopol* and *The Kreutzer Sonata* by Tolstoy in the camp library, and on the troopship I read *A Room with a View* by E. M. Forster, and *The Mutiny on the Elsinore* by Jack London. The fact that I remember the names of these books shows not only that they were 'memorable' in their content, but that it was rare for me to read a book at all.

At best it was random reading, and I couldn't much tell the difference between those books and *The Further Adventures of Jack the Ripper*—though the harder the book was (that is to say, the slower I was forced to read it) the more I was aware that I was getting something out of it. Certainly, those early books were unforgettable in the density they seemed to possess.

When I got back to England at twenty, and had to go into hospital with tuberculosis, the real reading started. You name it, I read it—in the following few years. One book which I latched on to in my hospital bed was *The Forest Giant* by Adrien le Corbeau, translated by T. E. Lawrence, and published by (I think) Jonathan Cape in the 'twenties. It was a slim book with rather nice woodcuts, a simple story of the birth and death of a tree by a river bank on the edge of a forest. It began as a minute seed falling from a mature tree and being washed down the river. Eventually it lodged on the bank and put out roots, and grew into an enormous 'forest giant' when the course of the river shifted. The book describes its life until, as a dying tree, it falls into the dust and bracken.

The book was speckled with 'meaningful' sentences, such as (if I remember correctly: I wrote many down at the time but have since lost the notebook): 'An incurable illness is a premature old age, and premature old age is an incurable illness.' Being, as far as I knew, incurably ill at the time (twenty-five thousand people a year died of tuberculosis in those days: it was almost like being told today that you have cancer), the sentence seemed profound and real to me. Maybe such a quotation is a bad example, however, and seems somewhat banal now, but at the time that sort of writing was new to me. It was satisfying to my mind. It was like going back to some well of pure water I'd inadvertently strayed from.

I've looked for *The Forest Giant* in bookshops, libraries, and all the houses I've entered, but have not found it. I'd be interested to read it again so as to see what attracted me to it, because it might indicate what my fluid half-formed mind was like at that time.

It is no use compiling a list of the books I enjoyed. There are too many—and they wouldn't necessarily be the ones that influenced me. Those I liked obviously took me on an escape route away from one reality, but into another that seemed more relevant to my own spirit, one which allowed me to keep a grip on my dreams. So I can mention *Nostromo, The Charterhouse of Parma, The Rainbow,* and *Moby Dick.*

Those books that influenced me are the fundamental texts that hit me, sank so deeply I hardly felt their hidden purpose at the time. Or, what was also true, they stayed with me—or comforted me—at a time of crisis. It's not often possible to say which books these were, because the effect of what I read in them only occurs to me many years after the crisis, rising up suddenly out of memory when I am not thinking about them, or when another hard knock is imminent.

I've named two books. The first, *Les Misérables,* took me through the prolonged crisis of childhood, the second helped me to manage the shock of my first illness when I thought I was going to die at twenty: I didn't care to go on living in a state of premature decrepitude. I recovered, as one might now, though it took nearly ten years, and I did it simply by ignoring the fact that I was ill—which is another kind of story.

In both cases I turned to a book and not to people, which must have some significance. The gift of literacy, and the universal accessibility of books, made a priest unnecessary. A self-educated sceptic is fairly independent in that respect.

Since I saw the devastating and healing importance of books it's not so strange that I decided to write one of my own.

I won't go into that particular vein, because this is about reading, not writing—though I've never known how to keep the two separate. Writing fed on reading at first, till I could more or less see the mechanics of it. Then the writing fed on imagination and, last of all, on life itself—a meandering that finally brought the head back to the tail. But it was a long training of ten years, from the age of twenty to nearly thirty—though I don't suppose this is so long when, as Robert Graves states in *The White Goddess*, a Druid-poet went through a twenty-one year apprenticeship.

During the middle part of my decade of learning I came across *Sand*—a forty-page story by Israel Joshua Singer, one of many gems in a fat and priceless paperback anthology of Yiddish stories. *Sand* is a simple and unostentatious tale of poor but religious people. They are rough and primitive and quarrelsome: 'After all, a human being is a human being and does human things'—the supreme sentence uttered when the inhabitants of Podgurna storm into the snootier and richer village of Grobitze to bring back the young man who has seduced the old Rabbi's granddaughter and make him marry her.

Reb Jonah, 'the elected rabbi and teacher and beadle and guide of Podgurna', had been taken off as a young man for twenty-five years' compulsory service in the Tsar's army, and in spite of all the torments and indignities did not deny his religious beliefs. He fought at Sevastopol and came back finally with three medals. In Siberia, where he was discharged, he had spent some years in the service of a village synagogue.

When the people of Grobitze made harsh conditions for those of neighbouring Podgurna about coming to worship in their synagogue and using their burial ground, the Podgurna people prevailed on Reb Jonah to become their rabbi.

This he does, though in a rather makeshift inefficient fashion regarding the tighter points of doctrine. He also runs the *cheder* (school) to teach the children Hebrew, and he marches them into his classroom like the old soldier he is.

And then Aaron, the travelling ritual slaughterer, recently widowed, comes by from Grobitze, and is put up at Reb Jonah's house. Aaron is well-versed in the order of feast-days and ritual, so Reb Jonah is glad to have him nearby to refresh his own hazy mind. But Aaron gets into Mashka's bed, and trouble between Grobitze and Podgurna breaks out once more.

The story is far more than this bare summary. It is rich, meandering, and somehow gets the whole of life in it—more than most novels, in fact. It is, to my mind, the jewel of Israel Joshua Singer's art—and I have since read all his novels and stories, as well as those of his younger brother, Isaac Bashevis Singer. Together they have erected a permanent monument to a great but (I'm grieved to say) vanished culture.

I feel that if I had not read *Sand* I should not have written *The Loneliness of the Long Distance Runner* (which I did some four years later) or *The Ragman's Daughter*, or *Mimic*. Or at least those stories would not have taken the *form* they did. *Sand* shows that much can happen between A and Z, that a tale is all the better—and richer—for being told in an unhurried, human and loving way. Not sentimental, but moving and respectful of life. A man should live, if only to satisfy his curiosity.

The tale, picked originally at random, led me to go through the rest of the book, to read *Kola Street, Repentance, Competitors*—and all the rest. From them I saw that the historians of hearts and souls were not indeed inferior to those of the historians of external facts. The two conditions seemed to meet in these stories, and though I already knew that they did so I was happy to find such supreme and consummate examples of it. I had found travelling companions at a time when I felt somewhat alone.

The best time for reading a good stylish story is in fact when one is on a train travelling alone. With strangers roundabout, and unfamiliar scenery passing by the window (at which you glance now and again) the endearing and convoluted life coming out of the pages possesses its own peculiar and imprinting effects. An author can't have you more firmly in his grip than when his tale has put out of your mind the rhythmical beating of train wheels. A good book, an absorbing story, stops time, and gives further distance to eyes that look inwards. And the greater distance in, the greater distance out.

And in the story called *Sand* we are taken through all the seasons of the lonely bone-poor settlement on the banks of the Vistula, and I can never forget the few lines in which the author describes the Russian cannon at the fort firing at the heaped-up ice-flows in spring, breaking them up so as to save the village from inundation—for which the inhabitants of Podgurna are touchingly grateful.

I have read *Sand* many times. It makes me feel good. I know the people in the story very well. When the women of Podgurna find out that Mashka has just given birth, they panic at the disgrace. Wondering what the self-righteous inhabitants of Grobitze will say, they flow into the humble Podgurnian synagogue during a service conducted by Mashka's, as yet unknowing, pious grandfather. But Pesach Plotnik, the community strongman, brings his meaty fist down on the pulpit and roars: 'Women and children, out of here! All of you, you bastards!'

Later he leads the foray against neighbouring Grobitze, to bring back the young Aaron who is made to marry Mashka. And at the wedding-feast you know they are going to be happy—well, as happy as a young married couple can be after a few years. All has ended well, but it needed a whole community to put things right.

Literature belongs to the world, not to one country. I felt I had met many of those people from *Sand* before, both in literature and in life. Those Yiddish stories are like a country I once lived in. I don't know why. The people are poor. They are vivid. They feel much. What's more, the authors who write about them love them. That alone makes you feel good. People do not live in classes or masses, nations or groups. They are all individuals. Every grain of sand is different. When I see a long stretch of sand along a sea shore or river bank I know that not one grain of sand is the same as any other, even though there are more than anybody can count.

So I place *Sand* with a few other great short stories. I'll make the following list to show what I mean:

Sand by Israel Joshua Singer.

A Gentleman from San Francisco by Ivan Bunin.

Heart of Darkness by Joseph Conrad.

Lenz by Georg Buechner.

Las Encantadas by Herman Melville.

The Steppe by Anton Chekhov.

If I had them in one book I would place it beside *Les Misérables* and the Old Testament, and row them to my desert island.

One more book before I finish. It is called *The Anatomy of Melancholy*—English, this time, if that means anything. Robert Burton wrote it, a seventeenth-century priest endlessly expatiating on sin, concupiscence, plague, illness, ghosts, servitude, hypochondria, passion, love, madness, melancholy, medicine, supersition, despair, lycanthropy and jealousy—drawing in hundreds of obscure authors and classical quotations, and linking them in the richest of English commentaries—witty, profound, often misanthropic, but always a treasure-house of rare words, original compounds, and far-out anecdotes. It is the sort of packed marvellous idiosyncratic prose that can quench anyone's thirst in the desert of life.

I would certainly stake my heart on that book as well, throw it in the boat to that hypothetical desert island even if it sank it.

Such people, such books, such prose make me, at certain times, happy to be alive, and even happier to be a writer. One is not often happy, but I can be so when I take up again those books that helped me to know for sure when I was happy because they were opening doors which I knew to exist, but to which I did not have the key till then.

ELIZABETH TAYLOR

The first of my reading was Beatrix Potter, although this may not have been proper reading, but remembering what had been read to me the night before. I certainly knew when to turn the page, and which pale picture matched the text. After that came two characters in a coloured primer —Fan and Ned—and then the Bruin Boys in *Rainbow*. I loved those animal characters—Tiger Tim, the hero, Jocy the Parrot, Porky Boy the pig, who never shared the goodies in his hamper. I can see now the picture of a cake with thick icing dripping down its side like candle-wax. When I was lying alone at night I envied them their communal, cheery bed, with little Joey on its precarious edge.

I am glad that I learned to read early. *Alice in Wonderland* was an extraordinary experience of dropping and floundering, of growing and diminishing; nothing like the cosy though patriotic world of *Little Folks*, a magazine I read at about the same time.

At school, the French books we studied were rather young for our ages because of our slow progress in the language. First came *Les Malheurs de Sophie*—that charming, naughty little girl with her formidable Mamma—and then *Capi et son*

Troupe, a world I was glad enough to enter on dull afternoons.

The English reading to me at school was terrible indeed—a dreaded business of *The Talisman* and *Ivanhoe* and *Hereward the Wake*. Jane Austen was compulsory reading too. It is a wonder that I did not miss *Mansfield Park*, as I missed *Ivanhoe*. Now, Jane Austen and Ivy Compton-Burnett are the writers to whom I most often return. Outside school-reading came the Brontës, their lives and their works linked vividly together for me. In late adolescence I was absorbed in, influenced by, Virginia Woolf and Katherine Mansfield, and nothing either did was ever wrong. Mary Webb has fared worse with me. No; she has not fared at all.

I have always read poetry much less than fiction, and even less now than when I was young—so little between the Bard and *Four Quartets*, and practically nothing since. When I was young, there was, of course, Rupert Brooke. Gazing at his photographed profile, I told myself that his poetry was good, too, though it was not necessary for it to be. I still think the profile beautiful. The last time my friend Elizabeth Bowen came to stay with us, she returned from the village second-hand bookshop with a volume of the *Letters of Rupert Brooke*. Showing it to me, she said, 'It was the first time I ever heard of Henry James.' And for me. The Master loomed (I believe that must be the word) into my world as some old codger Rupert Brooke had called upon at Rye.

I re-read funny books a great deal, because there seem to be so few of them. It is good to have something to dispel the terrors of the night—*The Young Visitors, The Diary of a Nobody, Decline and Fall, Lucky Jim, Potatoes are Cheaper*, by Max Shulman, *Billy Liar*. To be unable to stop laughing is invigorating, good for the circulation. Ivy Compton-Burnett can make me laugh aloud; but it may end in tears, as children are told.

Of foreign translations, I love those with a powerful sense of atmosphere, like *Le Grand Meaulnes, Madame Bovary*, Aksakov, Turgenev, the short stories and plays of Chekhov.

What has lasted? On my way up to bed I so often decide

that I am not in the mood to persevere with my library book, so I walk along the shelves wondering whether it shall be Ivy or Jane. The spines of my Martin Secker set of Jane Austen are faded and worn, but what an example of perfect shape, format, clarity the books are. If Jane had written just one more novel, I think, they would not come round again so quickly. So I should like more books to make me laugh—preposterous situation observed with gentle self-betrayal, perhaps. And I need one more Jane Austen novel. It might come between *Emma* and *Persuasion*—or anywhere else she could have fitted it in, conveniently to her dear self.

HUGH THOMAS

I am afraid that it will seem affected but the books which influenced me as a writer seem to me to have been French. I think this is because at the time when I began to regard myself as someone who desired to write I was just beginning to be able to appreciate French literature. This was in my second or third year at Cambridge, 1952 or 1953. I remember a friend of mine, now a professor of law, posting Heffer's last set of the Gallimard Proust to me in Avignon in the summer of 1952. I don't think I finished *Le Temps Retrouvé* until 1954 when I was living in Paris. But I must have read quite a lot of it between 1952 and 1953. I also read a great deal of French poetry and other French novels, particularly Flaubert, during this time, and it seems to me that this bout of francophilia was the most sustained piece of reading for pleasure (or out of ambition, as Flaubert would have believed) of my life. Other reading has usually been in connection with my books or my job or something similar.

There was one guidebook to French literature, I confess, which probably influenced me more than I would have liked then to have admitted—Connolly's *The Unquiet Grave*. I must have read that about ten times as an undergraduate and, of course, as well as being, as everyone admits, a little masterpiece of its own, it was a wonderful signpost and I think I followed most of the roads leading from it—would I have ever read Sainte Beuve, Chamfort, La Bruyère, even Baudelaire and Rimbaud without Connolly? I wonder.

You must be surprised that, having been so preoccupied by French literature, I have actually made my name as a historian and indeed as a historian of Spain, not France. This was accidental. I will freely admit that, having written a novel, *The World's Grave* (1957), I selfconsciously sought a theme for a historical work and found it in the Spanish war. Was I influenced by Gibbon's *Autobiography*, in which he describes how he tried first to write about the Medici, or the Swiss, or Sir Walter Raleigh? I should like to think so, but I'm not sure I really was. I remember reading, after I left Cambridge, Gerald Brenan's wonderful *The Spanish Labyrinth*, on the advice of Christopher Bennett, when I first went to Spain in December 1955; and I recall very well the impression that made on me. But that was intellectual, not artistic exactly. I'm afraid that I cannot think of any historians whose writings inspired me artistically, apart from those of the nineteenth century. The best work of history I read as an undergraduate was Eisenmann's magnificent study, *Le Compromis Austro-Hongrois de 1867*, long since out of print, which I remember reading on the recommendation in a bibliography of Alan Taylor. Alan Taylor I did find very exciting as an undergraduate. I must say I find today's undergraduates do so too.

Now I must get back to Hans Andersen, which I'm reading to my daughter ...

ARNOLD WESKER

Each One a Landmark

The trouble is—I forget. I could always remember that between the ages of seventeen and twenty I was absorbed by D. H. Lawrence, but I'd forget I'd read Lewis Mumford's *The Culture of Cities* or Herbert Read's *The Meaning of Art*. I know I've read Lytton Strachey's *Eminent Victorians* and Peter Quennell's books on Byron, but when? Was it before I went into the R.A.F. or after? *The Years of Fame* bears my name followed by 1954. But *Byron in Italy* bears nothing. I'm quite likely to have borrowed them from the library in 1950 and bought them four years later. And when did I read Silone's *Fontamara*, Colette's *Chéri*, Wilder's *The Bridge of San Luis Ray*, Waugh's *Brideshead Revisited*? Oh yes, Evelyn Waugh is the only writer one of whose books so grated offensively on my nerves that I was driven to tear it up half way through. But which one? And how old was I? There's a good guessing game! Yet don't I remember crying over *Brideshead*?

Of these things, though, I'm certain: that my beginnings were formed by *Just William*, *Morte d'Arthur*, *The Wind in the Willows*, *The Three Musketeers*, and the poetry of Louis MacNeice—especially *Autumn Journal*. *The Wind in the Willows* I read at least half a dozen times and cried through each time.

The Tales of Arthur, which I pored over endlessly, surely accounts for more of me than I care to acknowledge. At school I formed my own group of Musketeers of whom, naturally, I was D'Artagnan. And by fourteen I'd written my own *Journal of Spring and Summer*. From thirteen to sixteen I was learning political history and having basic socialist values formed by the novels of Upton Sinclair and Jack London with Sinclair Lewis, Howard Spring, Howard Fast and A. J. Cronin tucked in between. By the time I reached late teens Dostoyevsky, the Brontës, Turgenev, De Maupassant, Gorki and Hemingway were reaching out to me from my family's bookshelves and teaching me that man was very complex, sad and devious indeed. I stumbled across Thomas Hardy and E. M. Forster during conscription with the R.A.F. But, ashamedly, had to wait until my thirties and the dubious responsibilities of fame to discover Austen, Henry James, George Eliot, Balzac, Ruskin and Carlyle, at which point I believe my writing to have deepened and matured, and fame began hovering uncertainly.

But landmarks? Those special books which made special impressions? How do we know? I once planned to write a play on the life of Jesus, making him a natural and inevitable product of the Jewish personality. Surely the seeds for that lay in the reading of Renan's *Life of Jesus* and George Moore's *The Brook Kerith*? The Arthurein legends are deeply embedded in me, for good or ill, I'm not sure which. So is Howard Spring's *Fame is the Spur*; I could not have written *Their Very Own and Golden City* without it. But it's not a greater book than *Tess of the D'Urbervilles*, that's for sure. Impressions, then, must also have to do with what I knew instinctively would be fitting for me to write; I'd love to have written in the style of Hardy, we all would, but we write in our times, crippled and enriched, both.

Other landmarks? Landmarks of what? I read Salinger's *Catcher in the Rye* to my wife in bed and we were convulsed with laughter and made tender, as I imagine was a whole

Salinger generation. That gave, surely, a foundation to our relationship. When I read Gorki's *Decadence* I felt I understood how a novel was constructed. Aged what? The book bears the date 26/6/53. I was twenty-one. What a great way to become of age. I know I encountered for the first time the notion of a history of ideas after I'd read *To the Finland Station* by Edmund Wilson; and I know I was shattered and strengthened by a collection of essays which—despite their impact—I felt were mediocre as writing: *The God that Failed.* I was twenty.

But most vivid (slowly it comes back), the first of all the landmarks, while browsing at the age of fifteen in the reference room of Hackney Library, where I spent time swotting for the School Certificate I failed (perhaps too much browsing was the cause), and from whose shelves I picked a heavy volume called *An Anthology of World Poetry*, edited by Mark Van Doren, first published in 1929. Looking back I can't think why it should have been a revelation to me but suddenly, for the first time, I was aware that the Chinese wrote poetry. The English, Americans, French, Germans, even the Greeks (Ulysses had reached Hackney) and the Persians (I was composing my own tunes to the first verses of the *Rubàiyàt*), but the *Chinese* wrote poetry? The Chinese wrote *poetry*? And not only writing it but doing so five hundred years before Christ. The floodgates were open. Poem upon poem 'after the style of the Chinese' came out of me. It seemed easy. A mere recitation of the everyday. I could make them up as I spoke them, and many years passed before I learned about the need to juxtapose the right images. When I later worked in a bookshop, in 1953, I found a second-hand copy of that anthology and was prepared to pay a high price for it.

What did I weep over besides *The Wind in the Willows*? Ah! *Absalom O Absalom* by Spring, Hardy's *Jude the Obscure, Portrait of a Lady* by Henry James. But Doris Lessing's *A Proper Marriage* made me rush to spend my last pennies on flowers for my mother, and *Emma* made me respect the world again when I'd lost some love of it. But I never read plays, nor went to the theatre. Awareness of the acted-out experience came to me through the cinema and my membership of an amateur dramatic company. Somewhere in my plays must surely be found the greater influence of screen technique and the wide canvas of prose than conventional drama. *Chicken Soup With Barley* may be in the traditional three acts, but in spanning twenty years from 1936 to 1956 it attempts the sweep through time belonging more to the cinema and the novel. As I'm a playwright I suppose I must at least pause to observe this, while resisting the temptation to make that analysis of my work I wish others would make!

And what about those odd books, the enthusiasms of one's eccentric friends? I know that my brother-in-law introduced me to R. H. Mottram's *Spanish Farm* and the haunting *Odd John* of Olaf Stapledon; and who it was urged me to the strange *Nightwood* of Djuna Barnes, and Johnson's *Rasselas* and *A Voice through a Cloud* by the doomed Denton Welch: but who urged me to read Ivy Compton-Burnett or Helen Thomas's *As it Was* and *World without End* which I then used to buy for any and everyone? And how did Elliot Paul's *A Narrow Street* come into my life, and Arthur Morrison's *A Child of the Jago*?

Banal though it sounds, every good book is a unique experience, and when you are as impressionable as I am then each one is a kind of landmark. Lawrence's *Plumed Serpent* was difficult for me to read as a collection of ideas, but it didn't begin to exhaust me as did Virginia Woolf's *Orlando*. I could only take four pages of that at a time and when it was over I was stunned by it as by only one other book since: Doris Lessing's *The Four-Gated City*.

There is only one little book I owe to school: *The Albatross Book of Living Verse* edited by Louis Untermeyer and brought in by my sardonic, courageous and indulgent English master, Mr Walsh. I found Gerard Manley Hopkins there, and used to read—as warnings—to my girl-friends a poem called 'Four Preludes on Playthings of the Wind' by Carl Sandburg. And how my own verse was touched by the rhythms of Vachel Lindsay's 'The Kalliope Yell'.

As one reminisces on so, more is remembered. Of course! What about those beacons of hope and encouragement for the embryonic Jewish East-End writer: Willie Goldman's *East End My Cradle* and *The Light in the Dust*. I was in love with one of his nieces! And Israel Zangwill's *Children of the Ghetto*. Why, the novel opened in Fashion Street, where I actually lived!

Ambivalence is strongest, though, over the huge Irving Stone biographical novels of the great American political figures: *Darrow for the Defence, Sailor on Horseback* (about Jack London), and *Adversary in the House* (about Eugene V. Debs). I've just turned to look at the last page of this one—page 483:

> It was more than half a century since Lincoln's death, yet Gene had seen as much suffering and slavery as Lincoln had. The Negroes had been freed, or so the law said, but man had not freed them. The whites had been born free, or so the law said, but man kept them enslaved. Slavery, in its new machine form, was on the march, increasing with each fruitful discovery, each resourceful device.
>
> Had Lincoln worked in vain? He did not know. But Abraham Lincoln would not have forgone the struggle. The torch of liberty must somehow, in the darkness and the hurricane, be kept alive.
>
> 'It is not upon thee to finish the work; neither art thou free to desist from it.'
>
> Smiling at Theodore, he offered up to God the only prayer he knew: 'While there is a lower class I am in it. While there is a working class I am of it. While there's a soul in prison I am not free.'
>
> Slowly, he walked down the marble stairs.

I once swore to myself I'd never betray, or diminish in later life, what my innocent and vulnerable youth was; but that last page leaves me with very mixed feelings, especially when I think back on a novel like Eliot's *Felix Holt* which, though about a *fictional* political figure, is comparable and, by comparison, infinitely better.

> 'Hush, hush, my young friend,' said Mr Lyon, hurt by this levity, which glanced at himself as well as at the deacon. 'Play not with paradoxes. That caustic which you handle in order to scorch others may happen to sear your own fingers and make them dead to the quality of things. 'Tis difficult enough to see our way and keep our torch steady in this dim labyrinth: to whirl the torch and dazzle the eyes of our fellow-seekers is a poor daring, and may end in total darkness. You yourself are a lover of freedom, and a bold rebel against usurping authority. But the right to rebellion is the right to seek a higher rule, and not to wander in mere lawlessness. Wherefore, I beseech you, seem not to say that liberty is licence. And I apprehend —though I am not endowed with an ear to seize those earthly harmonies, which to some devout souls have seemed, as it were, the broken echoes of the heavenly choir—I apprehend—that there is a law in music, disobedience whereunto would bring us in our singing to the level of shrieking maniacs or howling beasts: so that herein we are well instructed how true liberty can be nought but the transfer of obedience from the will of one or of a few men to that will which is the norm or rule for all men. And though the transfer may sometimes be but an erroneous direction of search, yet is the search good and necessary to the ultimate finding. And even as in music, where all obey and concur to one end, so that each has the joy of contributing to a whole whereby he is ravished and lifted up into the courts of heaven, so will it be that crowning time of the millennial reign, when our daily prayer will be fulfilled, and one law shall be written on all hearts, and be the very structure of all thought, and be the principle of all action.'

Yet recently I read Peter Quennell's portrait of Ruskin. Stone may be wildly sentimental and absurdly heroic but he was generous, a quality all great writing contains, though of course not all writing that contains it is great, but I could barely stomach the begrudging, thin-lipped English tone of Quennell. How sad that a full-blooded literary passion has become diluted in this unhappy country, and the English tradition of cool but humane appraisal degenerated into put-downery. It chilled me to read (but couldn't finish) the biography of H. G. Wells by the Mackenzies. I trembled that my own poor faults and failures might one day fall into the hands of such gloating deprecators.

But look! Consider who I'd nearly forgotten: Aldous Huxley and his *Brave New World*. My God! And Stendhal and Rousseau and Scott Fitzgerald and Tolstoy, Chekhov, Joyce, Camus, Orwell. *Animal Farm* made me angry—it seemed so dishonestly contrived at the time—but the years passed and with their passing it grew to mean more and more. What other books were there like that? Those with images and meanings assuming greater significance as one lived and lived on? In *The Bridge of San Luis Rey* one of two brothers discovers that of two people who love, one always loves the least. Friendships assumed anxious shapes beneath perceptions like that. And Fitzgerald's *Tender is the Night*—that slow progress of the strong to destruction at the hands of the weak. I don't think I could have written *The Four Seasons* without it. And now, ominously, loom two other books into my consciousness: Orwell again, *1984*, with a world divided into three super powers; and Jack London's *Iron Heel*. Through literature I learned, very early on, that the impact of art is not immediate but cumulative. It takes time, the light hangs around until one's own moment of darkness comes. Hence, though my values will always be those of the left, yet I quarrel with their expectations of art.

Which made the greater impact upon me, the original Gospels or Rieu's new translation specially for Penguin Classics? Which did I read first, besides? And how can I forget the impact of *Candide* and *Madame Bovary* or—to plot the turning point of my career into a dramatist—Osborne's *Look Back in Anger*? Dylan Thomas! Thomas Wolfe! Walt Whitman! Now there, significantly, my love of literature gained impetus and strength. Three of the most disastrous teachers a writer could have. It took me years to write them out of my system. The roll call of honour could go on.

But—more depressing than the memory of those I've loved having made me, is the thought of those I've not read who could have made me better: Chaucer, Conrad, Dickens, Walter Scott, Meredith, Thackeray, Trollope, Sholem Asch, Goethe, Proust ... The list is intimidating but—there's time, with luck there's time.

RAYMOND WILLIAMS

There were very few books in our house when I was a child: all I remember are the *Bible,* the *Beekeeper's Manual, Hours with English Authors* (an anthology of extracts used in the evening class which my father attended), *The Wonder Book of Why and What* and a translation of Euripides' *Trojan Women* which my mother gave me for my birthday. Later, after I went to grammar school, there was a one-volume Shakespeare and a set of Dickens bought through a newspaper subscription (I think the *Daily Herald*).

I remember reading all these, with the kind of over-and-over reading I have never, with certain books, lost as a habit. What it meant, of course, as I can now see, is that I acquired a particular attitude to reading which in spite of everything I have not much changed. As my education continued I read for work: the set-books at school—Chaucer and Shakespeare and Milton and Blake and Wordsworth and Keats and Charlotte and Emily Brontë and Shaw; then, reading English at Cambridge, the historical range of English literature, with gaps which I went on filling when I began to teach the same range. What I read outside work was, from the initial situation, a very small and curious selection.

At a certain stage, in my late twenties, the definition of reading for work altered. From that time on, it was my own work, and for about half of my books this required really massive reading programmes. From about 1946 to 1950 there was the systematic reading of all the modern European drama I could find: the reading that went into *Drama from Ibsen to Eliot* and *Drama from Ibsen to Brecht*. My reading of Ibsen, especially, was like the childhood reading: over-and-over, as if no other books were available. But although this was my own project, it had evident continuities with my academic studies. The only other book I have written of which this has been true is *The English Novel from Dickens to Lawrence*, which came directly out of lecturing and belonged to a later stage of reading over-and-over, with George Eliot and Hardy and Lawrence, especially, the writers I read as if no other books existed.

That side of my reading is then easily described. But it isn't the whole of my reading for work. The sort of reading I had to do for, say, *Culture and Society* and *The Country and the City* was in each case a matter of some six or seven years, steady work, along lines I had almost wholly to devise for myself. It meant, in each case, a break beyond the usual reading lists: in particular a combination, which is now much more familiar, of books conventionally separated into the categories of literature, history, social philosophy, sociology. A lot of this went also into the second part of *The Long Revolution*.

These parts of my reading are then easily traced. In that kind of book the record of response and influence is direct. But there are two other kinds of writing for which I haven't, in effect, read at all, and in which I have even taken some pains not to read beyond what I already knew. I have written a good deal of what is called social and political philosophy: the first part of *The Long Revolution* is only the most obvious case; the conclusion of *Culture and Society* is another. Here I can see, looking back, a deliberate cut-off from reading, for a particular reason. For by this time I believed that what I had to do was to get out from under the received habits of thought that came with the received reading. This risked a certain awkward strangeness, a naïveté, which were indeed, in the first conventional responses, registered and assigned to me. But I have still to insist how deliberate it was. I was not part of orthodox English culture and social thought: not because it had not been made available to me but because I had seen it and did not want it. This remains true. Indeed it becomes more true with each year that passes.

The same thing is true, though in some different ways, with my novels. I wrote *Border Country* seven times, and during those years I read hardly any other novels. It was only after it was finished that I read George Eliot and Hardy and Lawrence repeatedly: in part for other reasons, in part to try to work out, with my own limited experience to hand, why the next kind of imaginative writing had to be different. *Second Generation* was a move in a quite different direction; I still find it significant that it didn't connect with other people's reading and has remained, in England though not in some other countries, quite isolated. Since the mid-'sixties I have been working and reworking a novel called *The Volunteers*. Here again I keep rather away from the nearest kind of reading. The English block on the interaction of what are called 'private' and 'public' experiences only increases my difficulties, whenever I come across it expressed, or expressed by an absence of attention to it, in works with some of the same apparent sources. I read, because they are at a distance, Sartre, Yashar Kemal, Solzhenitsyn, Grass, and some of the science-fiction writers—Vonnegut, for example—who use that form in its only interesting way: to explore the consequences of temporal discontinuity and historical breaks. Imaginative writing without that consciousness, which of course preoccupies me, I do not now read.

One final observation. The relative lack of books in my childhood had certain advantages which of course are still represented to me as disadvantages. I didn't read *Alice in Wonderland* or the English children's standard authors. I have since read most of them, but their absence led to a discontinuity with the tones and assumptions of many of my most literate contemporaries: in small ways, obviously; perhaps in larger ways. Another effect is that I have always done a lot of my reading on any available print: local newspapers, gardening catalogues, the *Radio Times* before it had articles. I still do that kind of reading, in periods of relaxation, as if nothing else were available. The effect is more marked now that I don't read any national newspapers or magazines, at least those published in this country. I get sent, from all over, underground papers, duplicated bulletins, distant offprints, unpublished manuscripts: I find them, as a body, very much more congenial and interesting. Meanwhile there is always reviewing, but there, these days, I can pick and choose, on the simple if hardly universal principle of taking books I want to read and then do actually read. That makes quite enough.